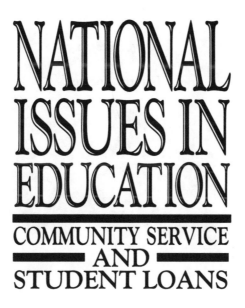

NATIONAL ISSUES IN EDUCATION

COMMUNITY SERVICE
━ AND ━
STUDENT LOANS

John F. Jennings, Editor

Published by
Phi Delta Kappa International
Bloomington, Indiana
and
The Institute for Educational Leadership
Washington, D.C.

Cover design
by
Victoria Voelker

Library of Congress Catalog Card Number 94-65876
ISBN 0-87367-466-9
Copyright © 1994 by Phi Delta Kappa and
The Institute for Educational Leadership

Table of Contents

Preface

Phi Delta Kappa and the Institute for Educational Leadership are pleased to co-publish *National Issues in Education: Community Service and Student Loans*. The purpose of this volume, the second in the National Issues series, is to present diverse perspectives on current major national education issues. Like the first volume, *National Issues in Education: The Past Is Prologue*, our goal is to focus on how major education issues have played out and will play out in the legislative process in the U.S. Congress.

This volume follows the community service and student loan issues as they recently proceeded through Congress. In articulating their diverse positions and perspectives, the authors of these essays illuminate the policymaking process by explaining the evolution of important new national policies and by tracing the history of these two significant pieces of legislation.

The issues on which this volume focuses reflect major policy priorities in the ambitious education agenda promulgated by the Clinton Administration. The community service concept enjoys widespread public bipartisan support, and all Americans are concerned about the burgeoning costs of postsecondary education.

We would once again like to thank John F. (Jack) Jennings, general counsel for education, Committee on Education and Labor, U.S. House of Representatives, for conceiving this joint venture and for his continued willingness to serve as editorial coordinator for this publication. We marvel at his ability to persuade prominent (and very busy) individuals from both inside and outside government to contribute their diverse perspectives to these volumes.

We repeat our hope that this volume, like its predecessor in this series, will be used in classrooms throughout the country, as well as for general discussion among educators, policy makers, business and political leaders, and others interested in the shaping of education policy in our nation's capital.

> Douglas Bedient
> President, Phi Delta Kappa
>
> Michael D. Usdan
> President, The Institute for Educational Leadership

Introduction

By John F. Jennings

In the years ahead, millions of Americans who wish to perform community service or to pursue education and training beyond high school will be affected by the creation in 1993 of the national community service program and by the massive overhaul in the same year of the federal student loan programs. The primary purpose of this book is to explain in the words of the main decision-makers these significant new national policies affecting education and to give the reasons that these changes were made.

The secondary purpose of this publication is to use the occasion of these changes to illuminate how policy is made at the national level. To many people, Washington, D.C., seems very far away; and the methods used in the nation's capital for deciding issues seem mysterious. This book is the second in a series being published by Phi Delta Kappa and the Institute for Educational Leadership. Both books have been designed to demystify the policy process. Americans ought to understand how their government sets policy so that they can influence the decisions being made at the national level.

The first book in the series was *National Issues in Education: The Past Is Prologue*, published in April 1993. That publication reviewed the discussions on education that occurred at the national level in 1991 and 1992, the last two years of the administration of President George Bush.

Those years were important in marking a change in the national perspective on education. President Bush and the state governors wrote the first-ever national goals for education, which implied that there was a much greater importance given to education at the national level than previously. To underscore that shift in thinking, the President, the governors, the major national education organizations, and the nation's major business groups endorsed the development of national content standards for education, moving away from the two-century-old American tradition of local control of education. As part of this expanding national interest in education, Congress grappled with bills to broaden federal aid to education to improve schooling for all children. And significant reforms in postsecondary student-aid programs also were debated.

In sum, the Bush years were significant in showing the beginnings of these important changes; but they were not noteworthy for bringing any of these reforms to a successful conclusion. The first book in this series explains this lack of success.

In 1993 President Bush was succeeded by Bill Clinton, who brought the Democrats back to the White House after it had been occupied by the Republicans for 12 years. But after defeating Bush in the elections, Clinton did not throw out all the ideas in education that Bush had advocated.

Instead, President Clinton endorsed the national goals for education, which, as governor of Arkansas, he had helped to write. He also encouraged the development of national content standards, which had begun under President Bush; and he submitted school reform legislation to the Congress, broadening federal aid to assist in improving education for all children. Clinton differed most significantly from Bush in opposing large-scale aid to private schools.

President Clinton is maintaining the shift in thinking about the national interest in education that began in the Bush years. But, having a much more activist view of the role of the federal government than did Bush, Clinton is expanding the way that the government will encourage this new thinking.

For instance, Clinton's school reform legislation, *Goals 2000: Educate America Act*, advocates a systemwide approach to improving education at the state and national levels, whereas Bush's approach talked about standards for all children but provided funds to improve only a handful of schools. Clinton also has submitted legislation to reform the array of current federal aid programs, principally the Chapter 1 program, to bring them more into line with a standards-driven, systemic approach. Further, he has submitted a bill to encourage the states to develop statewide school-to-work systems; and legislation will be submitted to reform Head Start and other federal programs.

Other books in this series will review developments regarding school reform, school-to-work, and other federal aid programs. This volume concentrates on decisions affecting community service and the federal loan programs that encourage people who wish to pursue postsecondary education and training.

In the arena of community service, Clinton showed a much more activist attitude than Bush. The former President in his inaugural speech spoke of a "thousand points of light" that he hoped would dot America. By this, he meant that many citizens were volunteering to work on projects in their communities, and he wanted to encourage this type of activity. Once in office, he created a national foundation to give awards to local community projects that encouraged this volunteerism; but he resisted a larger federal role in this area.

Clinton, during his campaign for the Presidency, also spoke of the value of volunteerism; but, being more activist than Bush, he pledged to create as a centerpiece of his administration a community service program to encourage millions of Americans to volunteer in their communities. He wanted to use the government, through a program of grants, to stimulate this volunteerism; whereas Bush was adverse to creating a federal program for this purpose and, therefore, preferred to give out awards and recognitions.

But the difference between the two men does not stop there. Clinton expanded on the concept of volunteerism by incorporating the notion that an individual could donate time for community service for a year or two and thus receive credit toward the cost of postsecondary education or training. In other words, he wove into the debate about volunteerism the idea that one could find a way to pay for further education or training while doing good service.

Americans have become increasingly concerned about the expanding costs of postsecondary education and their own shrinking ability to afford these expenses for their children or for themselves. Clinton's concept of earning one's way to a postsecondary education proved to be popular. Clinton claimed that his discussions of these ideas during the campaign brought forth more applause from audiences than any other ideas.

Once he assumed office, Clinton set to work to write a program that would incorporate these ideas. However, because of financial pressures related to the growing national debt, he faced difficulties in finding the resources to pay for these ideas. Thus a specific reform of the student-aid programs — shifting the federal student loan programs so that the federal government provided the funds for loans directly instead of using such intermediaries as banks and secondary loan markets — joined the legislative mix. The reason this idea was attractive was that billions of dollars could be saved by eliminating the "middle-men," the banks and secondary markets. These savings then could be redirected to pay for a community service program and for giving credits to those volunteers who wanted to pursue further education or training.

Reforming student-aid programs was attractive to Clinton not only because it raised the funds to pay for community service but also because it signified a philosophical shift toward helping people to pay for college only if they gave something back, namely service to their communities. As governor of Arkansas, Clinton had been active in the Democratic Leadership Conference that advocated such a shift as a means of changing government-aid programs so that recipients could assume more responsibility.

These ideas had been debated in Congress for several years, especially during the reauthorization of the Higher Education Act that occurred in the last two years of the Bush Administration. President Bush and Congress had battled during 1991 and 1992 over the idea of having the federal government become the primary maker of student loans, instead of subsidizing the banks and secondary credit markets to perform that role. A compromise had been fashioned in 1992 that authorized an experiment involving several hundred postsecondary institutions that were to begin in 1994 to offer loans provided by the federal government.

Once Clinton assumed office, he advocated moving the policy beyond the experimental stage to a full-fledged overhaul of the program, totally eliminating the banks and secondary markets. A fuller understanding of the battle over direct lending that occurred between the Bush Administration and Congress and of the proposed experiment can be obtained by reading the first book in this series, *National Issues in Education: The Past Is Prologue*. That background will be helpful in reading the five essays on direct lending in this book.

President Clinton submitted legislation to Congress to implement these ideas: community service, credits for education, and direct lending of student loans. This legislation was put into two packages, one dealing with community service and credits for education and a second one dealing with direct lending of student loans. The two packages were interrelated. However, given the way that Congress deals with issues, it was decided that they should be separated, as will be explained later.

This book follows these two pieces of legislation as they were written and then passed through the Congress. The first set of ideas was dealt with as a separate bill and progressed through the House and Senate on its own track to be finally enacted as the National and Community Service Trust Act of 1993. The second set of changes was incorporated into the legislation establishing the budget for the federal government for the five years, 1994-1998. This bill became the Omnibus Budget Reconciliation Act of 1993 and is commonly known as the deficit reduction bill.

Congress deals quite differently with a regular bill, such as the community service bill, and with a budget bill, such as the one incorporating the student loan changes; therefore, readers will be able to see the different mix of legislative rules and their effects on the outcomes in these two bills. Readers also will see how the politics surrounding these two bills came together at the end of the legislative process and how decisions on one bill had an effect on the other.

So Clinton's ideas of community service, credits for education, and direct lending of student loans were united when he made his proposal because they were complementary. Then they were divided in the Congress because of legislative and political reasons and proceeded on separate courses. In the end, legislative considerations of the bills on separate tracks became intertwined and decisions on one bill affected policymaking on the other.

The first part of this book will deal with the first bill: community service and credits for education. The second part of the book will describe the related legislation reforming the federal student loan programs. The last chapter will show the connection between the two bills and will draw lessons about the decision-making process in Washington from how these two bills became law.

Parts I and II follow the same format. Part I begins with an official from the Clinton Administration describing the policy that the President advocated, how it was formed, and how the Administration secured congressional enactment of the ideas. Eli Segal presents this perspective on community service, since he headed the office on community service in the White House in 1993. Segal is now the chief executive officer of the Corporation for National and Community Service, which is administering the new program. In Part II, Madeleine Kunin presents the Administration's views on direct lending of student loans, since she is the Deputy Secretary of Education in the U.S. Department of Education and was a leader in the formulation of Clinton Administration policy on student aid.

The next paper in each of the two parts of this book is presented by the principal advocate of the proposals in Congress. In Part I, Senator Edward Kennedy of Massachusetts discusses the community service bill, since he was the principal sponsor of that legislation in the Senate. In Part II, Congressman William Ford of Michigan describes the passage of the direct lending legislation in the House of Representatives, since he was the prime sponsor of that bill in the House. Both these members of Congress are Democrats and the chairmen in their respective houses

xi

of the legislature of the committees that have responsibility for education, training, and labor issues.

Following the Democrats in each part are the ranking Republican members of the same committees. Since the Democrats control the House and the Senate, these two individuals are the leaders of the minority party on those committees. In Part I, Senator Nancy Kassebaum of Kansas was an opponent of the Clinton community service bill in the Senate and wrote her own alternative to that legislation. In Part II, Congressman William Goodling of Pennsylvania led the opposition in the House to the Clinton proposal for direct lending of student loans.

The fourth essay in each part is written by an individual outside the government who was influential in advocating the ideas that became law. In Part I, this individual is Roger Landrum, president of Youth Service America, who is considered one of the leading experts in the country on the issue of community service; he was called on frequently for advice by the Clinton Administration and by supporters of the concept in Congress. In Part II, this individual is Thomas Butts, the associate vice-president for government relations of the University of Michigan, who was a forceful advocate for direct lending of student loans and a principal leader of the coalition working for the enactment of this reform during the congressional consideration of this bill in 1993.

The last essay in each part is written by an influential opponent of each of the two Clinton proposals. Part I includes Douglas Bandow, an expert with the Cato Institute in Washington, D.C., who has written extensively about community service and became a source of intellectual inspiration to those in Congress opposing the community service bill. Part II includes John Dean, an attorney working in Washington, who was a leader in the coalition of organizations opposing the Administration's direct lending legislation and who has represented the Consumer Bankers of America for several years.

The purpose in asking these particular individuals to contribute essays was to afford an opportunity for some of the principal actors in these policy dramas to give their perspectives on what happened and why it happened. Some of them were more involved than others and, clearly, some were more influential than others; but it is useful to have all the major points of view represented so that readers can see the range of competing views on these issues.

President Clinton won on both issues; but in the process of winning, he and his allies had to make significant concessions to the opponents of these ideas. This book allows the representatives of the President's

Administration to set forth his proposals and then lets the winning advocates in Congress give their reasons for their victories. It also includes the opponents, so that readers can understand why and how the proposals were changed before their enactment was secured.

I would like to thank Phi Delta Kappa and the Institute for Educational Leadership for agreeing to publish this series. The policies that are set in Washington have an effect on millions of people, and yet too frequently the reasons for these policies are not completely understood. This series gives those of us who are involved in making these decisions an opportunity to explain the issues before memories are lost and individuals move on to other pursuits. We hope that our work will make the decision-making process more understandable so that citizens will become more involved in these issues.

PART I
COMMUNITY SERVICE

Toward the Reality of National Service

By Eli Segal

Eli Segal is Assistant to the President and Chief Executive Officer of the Corporation for National and Community Service. He was formerly the Chief of Staff of the Clinton-Gore campaign, overseeing day-to-day operations, including planning, personnel, accounting, and finance matters. Mr. Segal served in a similar capacity as Chief Financial Officer during the presidential transition period.

Prior to the campaign, Mr. Segal owned and served as chief executive officer of several consumer product companies. Most recently, he was president of Bits & Pieces, Incorporated, a Boston-based direct marketer of puzzles, games, and gifts, which he founded in 1984. He also was the publisher of GAMES, a consumer magazine covering the world of puzzles.

A native of Brooklyn, New York, Mr. Segal received his bachelor's degree from Brandeis University in 1964 and a Juris Doctorate from the University of Michigan Law School in 1967. He is married and has two children.

When President Clinton walked across the White House lawn on 21 September 1993, flanked by members of youth corps from around the country, the crowd of more than 1,000 distinguished guests rose to its feet in a spontaneous ovation. They had come to see President Clinton sign the National and Community Service Trust Act of 1993 into law.

This was not the first time that the vision of service had inspired such applause. In fact, throughout Bill Clinton's 1992 campaign for the Presidency, which was supposed to be about "the economy, stupid," it was the idea of national service — of citizens working together to solve the nation's pressing problems, to build a spirit of community,

3

and to renew the American ethic of civic responsibility — that inspired the American people to cheer.

In drafting the national service bill, we drew on that enthusiasm at the grassroots of America. We looked to the history of service, as old as America itself. But we also followed the principles of reinventing government to which the Administration is deeply committed, because we believe that those principles will work, that they are the path to a better America. In this way, AmeriCorps — as the national service program was christened on the day of the bill signing — incorporates the legacy of the past, the needs of the present, and the promise of the future.

The Great Tradition of Service

In his campaign book, *Putting People First*, Governor Clinton described his national service proposal as a combination of the best of its two most direct ancestors: the GI Bill and the Peace Corps. The former offered an educational reward for service to the country; the latter capitalized on the idealism and energy of America's young people who were willing — indeed, eager — to fly to unknown lands because they believed that they could make a difference.

Later, then-Governor Clinton identified Franklin D. Roosevelt's Civilian Conservation Corps as another important national service model. The CCC of the 1930s engaged unemployed youth in conserving natural resources and building roads and trails. Begun as a temporary work-relief effort, the CCC ran for nine years and engaged more than three million young men in community service.

The President's program, then, had several identifiable precedents. But in a broader sense, the ancestry of national service is too broad and too deep to trace. Service programs like Big Brothers/Big Sisters date back to the turn of the century, while the larger tradition of service is as old as the very notion of American community.

For Bill Clinton, as for so many of his generation, John F. Kennedy made the difference. Kennedy set the modern service movement in motion in his inaugural address, when he told Americans to ask what they could do for their country. That challenge also set in motion the public service career of a young, Southern idealist named Bill Clinton.

As a result of Kennedy's challenge, in the first 32 years of the Peace Corps' existence more than 140,000 young people, all of them college graduates and most of them members of the middle class, served in 92 foreign countries. Through their service, they met critical needs in those countries: providing health care and agricultural assistance,

4

implementing such environmental reforms as reforestation projects, and promoting cross-cultural understanding both abroad and at home.

The Peace Corps experience changed the life of every one of its participants, broadening their cultural understanding and their sense that they were a part of something much, much greater than themselves. For them, and for those of us who followed their experiences from back home, the idea took hold. It became the seed of a national service initiative that was still three decades in the future.

A few years after the Peace Corps began, VISTA (Volunteers in Service to America) was founded and began providing thousands of volunteers every year to serve low-income communities throughout the United States. The 1960s also spawned new service opportunities for older Americans, including the Foster Grandparent Program and the Retired and Senior Volunteer Program (which, by the start of the new decade, would develop both a new name — the Older American Volunteer Programs — and a new brainchild — the Senior Companion Program). These important programs were administered by ACTION, the Domestic Volunteer Service Agency.

The 1970s and 1980s were in many ways a dark time for service at the national level, but a few individuals in both government and academe kept the vision of service alive.

Meanwhile, community-based service movements were experiencing just the opposite phenomenon. Such national nonprofit organizations as Youth Service America, the National Association of Service and Conservation Corps, the Campus Outreach Opportunity League, and Campus Compact began to promote a wide range of service opportunities for young people. In the two decades before President Clinton's election, local efforts gave birth to youth corps like the Los Angeles Conservation Corps, New York's City Volunteer Corps, and City Year, the youth corps programs that would be models for the national youth service initiative.

In 1990 the tide of the "me" era in government began to turn. The United States Congress passed the National and Community Service Act, setting up the Commission on National and Community Service. With strong bipartisan support, the commission in its two-year existence awarded $150 million in grants to programs that involved thousands of Americans of all ages and backgrounds in community service. These programs engaged students in community service projects that related to their classes, involved youth in conservation efforts, and put students into classrooms and hospitals to serve as aides, tutors, mentors, and companions.

Pillar of the Presidency

Wherever Bill Clinton went in his 1992 campaign for the Presidency, he talked about national service. He mentioned it in his announcement speech in October 1991; in his campaign book, *Putting People First*; at every stop on his campaign bus tour; and on every college campus. And he discussed national service in his inaugural address, where he challenged "a new generation of Americans to a season of service."

Wherever Bill Clinton mentioned national service, the response was the same: The audience broke into spontaneous, enthusiastic applause.

Why was the response to service so strong?

First, national service appealed to the very ideals on which the United States of America was built. Foremost among these ideals are three that Bill Clinton adopted as the major themes of his campaign: opportunity, responsibility, and community.

Our ancestors came to America without means, without a common language, and without family to provide a better future for their children. America was the land of opportunity where everyone, regardless of background, had a chance at a better life.

National service promised to make open to Americans an opportunity that many had lost: the opportunity to go to college. Today, because of the skyrocketing cost of higher education, more and more middle-class Americans are unable to send their children to college.

Candidate Clinton saw that this trend was having a disastrous effect on both our families' present and our nation's future. Through his national service proposal and a proposal to make repayment of loans contingent on income, young people would have the chance to borrow money to go to college and to pay that money back through service to their communities.

Service also appealed to the American ideal of responsibility — the old idea that you don't get something for nothing. With the rights and privileges of citizenship come responsibilities. So, too, with the right to a college education should come the responsibility to give something back, through the hard and necessary work of community service, to the community that provided that opportunity.

Finally, national service appealed to the American ideal of community. Despite the American myth of the "self-made man," Americans have always achieved the most success by helping each other. They always have understood that this is the way to build a barn, to build a trail, to build a community, to build a strong and free society. Strengthening community through service, by getting things done at the grassroots level, would become the core of the new service initiative.

In addition to its ideological appeal, Americans saw national service as a real solution to common social goals. A new "domestic Peace Corps" would help to mitigate the skyrocketing cost of higher education. By bringing diverse people together to work toward a common goal, service would help to strengthen the ties that bind us together as a people, across divisions in race, religion, ethnicity, gender, age, physical ability, sexual orientation, and political party.

And, most important, national service would get things done, effecting real and lasting change in American communities. It would make our schools stronger, our environment cleaner, our citizens healthier, and our streets safer.

Candidate Clinton promised that if he was elected, he would help provide Americans with the opportunity to pay for college through community service. Once elected, he set about to keep that promise and to do so in a way that both built on tradition and reflected the changing character of the federal government.

From Promise to Law

During the transition into the Clinton Presidency, we began to translate the vision of national service into law. We wanted to use what was good about old service programs, but we also were determined to make our program different. Our goal was to engage a broader spectrum of Americans; to produce better, faster, and more lasting results without creating a new federal bureaucracy; and to renew the ethic of service among all Americans.

The most important change in the national service initiative during the presidential transition was transforming the program from what might have appeared to be a loan forgiveness program aimed primarily at middle-class college graduates to a much larger service initiative.

As we began to develop the national service plan, it became clear that for national service to succeed, it had to be a truly national program. So we clarified our definition of who could serve to include all college-aged youth, whether they had just graduated from high school and wanted to serve before enrolling in college, or intended to attend vocational school after high school, or were not sure they were going to pursue higher education at all.

We also expanded the range of participants on the other end of the spectrum, making the program available to any American who was "young in spirit" and willing to make a substantial commitment to service in exchange for educational opportunity.

The transition's national service team also identified some basic structural elements of the plan. Rather than running programs directly, the corporation would invest in strengthening local nonprofit organizations already working to meet their communities' most urgent needs.

The corporation would fund programs through the establishment of bipartisan state commissions, giving a portion of its funding directly to states on a population-based formula. Additional funds would be administered to states on a competitive basis. The remaining dollars would be reserved for direct funding to a range of other programs run by nonprofit organizations, including cabinet-level agencies and multi-state partnerships.

The team also decided on four issues on which to concentrate the efforts of our national service initiative: health, public safety, the environment, and education.

We still had a long way to go to define our program's purpose, goals, and character. Fortunately, we'd have a lot of help along the way.

With a Lot of Help from Our Friends

Perhaps national service's most radical departure from the history of American law-making was this: We didn't go to Congress with a drafted bill. We wanted national service to be a partnership from the very beginning. We did this not out of modesty, but out of selfishness. First, we knew that the input of Congress would make our bill stronger. Second, we wanted Congress to be committed to the legislation; and we knew that the best way to foster commitment to the program was to involve Congress in creating it. With congressional support, we knew our bill would do more for service participants and the communities they would serve.

We worked closely with the staff of the Senate Committee on Labor and Human Resources and the House Committee on Education and Labor. We conducted outreach to the constituents of these committees. We asked people: What are your concerns about national service? What are your service dreams? How can we make national service work for you.

We met with labor representatives to ensure that our bill contained strong measures against displacement of full-time workers. And we worked with the higher education community to make them understand that we shared their concerns about campus aid and that our national service program would not compete for those financial aid funds. We made sure that national service would not only be national in product, but national in process.

8

This kind of collaboration meant compromise. National service emerged from the legislative process a more modest program. We reduced the size of the educational award from the original $6,500 to $5,000. We did this both to allow for broader participation in the program and to affirm our growing determination that national service be about an ethic of responsibility, not monetary gain.

We also reduced the overall size of our program to ensure that it would grow slowly and effectively from the grassroots, without bureaucracy and without interfering with the Administration's pressing budgetary concerns.

These compromises did not diminish our vision for national service; they enhanced it. In the end, we had a program that could capture the imaginations and the unique resources of Americans in all their diversity and in all their strength.

What America Got Out of the Deal

At his inauguration, the President called Americans to a season of service. The new corporation, signed into law in September 1993, will support service opportunities for Americans in all the seasons of life.

The early years will be a season of service. We will expand Serve-America programs to support service learning, an educational method that takes students into their communities to serve and brings them back to the classroom to learn from that service.

Young adulthood will be a season of service. The President's original vision for service was expanded, but at its core remains the idea of a program to provide opportunities for college-age youth to serve. To serve in AmeriCorps, one thing is required: a commitment to making a difference. In this program, Americans of all ages and backgrounds will come together and dedicate at least 1,700 hours of their time to strengthening American communities.

Most of them will serve directly in nonprofit programs already working to meet unmet environmental, health, public safety, and education needs at the local level. Some others will choose to serve outside their communities, in the areas of greatest need, perhaps through the VISTA component of the President's program. And still others will choose community service as an alternative to military service, serving in the corporation's new Civilian Community Corps.

In exchange for service, AmeriCorps participants will receive an education award of $4,725 for every term of service they perform.

The middle years of life will be a season of service. We know that a government program alone is not the answer. We need the support of the 94 million Americans, many of them working people, who devote a few hours of their time every week to service. Our corporation will not supplant their activities. We will supplement them.

And the later years of life, when people often find themselves again with more time to give, will be a season of service. The corporation will expand programs for older Americans, including Senior Companions, Foster Grandparents, and the Retired and Senior Volunteer Programs.

In expanding our program to include every season of life, the corporation aims to foster a spirit of civic responsibility among citizens, so that America will again be a land of opportunity, responsibility, and community.

The Greatest Success, The Greatest Work

Through a broad, bipartisan effort in both drafting our bill and shepherding it through committees and debates, the National and Community Service Trust Act of 1993 passed through Congress with record support and in record time. Just eight months after he took office, President Clinton walked across the South Lawn of the White House with youth corps members from all over America to sign the bill into law, creating the Corporation for National and Community Service.

President Clinton championed Congress' passage of national service legislation as one great success of his first year in office. And though it was indeed an important victory, the real work of creating a national service movement is still before us.

The success of the new movement will depend on three things:

1. Quality programs. There are several things that the corporation will do to ensure that it funds quality programs. First, we will demand that corporation programs get things done. A year after the first funding announcements are made (expected to be in spring of 1994), we will return and evaluate the program by rigorous standards, demanding that they show results.

We will continue to develop our national priority areas, defining specific goals within education, health, public safety, and the environment.

We will encourage public-private partnerships, so that corporations increasingly realize that stronger communities mean better business.

We will make sure that every state sets up a strong state commission on national service to review and recommend programs for funding.

We will provide technical assistance and training, both to program directors and to program participants.

2. Community involvement. Without real, dedicated community involvement, national service will be a bitter disappointment. That is why we will make sure that state commissions are strong and citizen-driven. That is why, in the first year of operation, every nonprofit organization that applies to the corporation for funding will have to raise at least 25% of its program costs and at least 15% of the minimum-wage stipend that participants will earn at the local level. That is why we require that our programs do work that the community believes in and is willing to sustain.

3. Individual commitment. The units of success are even smaller. The government can create a program and encourage community support. It can steer the national service initiative toward success. But the real work — the rowing — must be done by individuals. Martin Luther King Jr. said that "everyone can be great because everyone can serve." The success of our initiative will require not only community involvement, but individual commitment on the part of every service participant.

President Clinton recognized this at the bill-signing ceremony when he said: "It is at the grassroots, in the heart of every citizen that we will succeed or fail . . . more and more and more we will all understand that we must go forward together. This is the profoundest lesson of this whole endeavor."

As early as September 1994, school-age youth in service learning programs, traditional volunteers, and participants in the senior volunteers programs will be joined by 20,000 AmeriCorps members on the streets and in the schools. Together, we will work throughout the seasons of life to make our country healthy, literate, safe, and free.

Enacting the National and Community Service Trust Act of 1993

By Senator Edward M. Kennedy

Edward M. Kennedy has represented the Commonwealth of Massachusetts in the United States Senate since 1962. He was educated at Harvard University, the International Law School at The Hague, and the University of Virginia Law School. Senator Kennedy has been chairman of the Senate Committee on Labor and Human Resources since 1987. He was the chief sponsor and floor manager of the National and Community Service Trust Act of 1993 and introduced and floor-managed the National and Community Service Act of 1990.

He also serves as a member of the Judiciary, Armed Services, and Joint Economic Committees in the Senate. Senator Kennedy has received numerous awards for his efforts to reform America's education and health care systems, strengthen civil rights, and promote nuclear disarmament.

At critical moments in the nation's history, Americans have found solutions to their problems in a renewed commitment to serving others. In the 1930s, faced with the most severe depression in United States history, President Franklin D. Roosevelt established the Civilian Conservation Corps and the Works Progress Administration to promote public service while providing opportunities for millions of the unemployed. In the 1960s, as the country was fighting communism abroad and poverty at home, President John F. Kennedy established the Peace Corps to reach out to the peoples of the world, and President Lyndon B. Johnson created Volunteers in Service to America (VISTA) to serve in low-income urban and rural areas.

As the nation entered the 1990s, it became clear that once again there was strong popular support for a new national service initiative. With state and local governments struggling to meet a host of growing social needs, many communities were turning increasingly to volunteers and civic organizations to shore up overburdened public services. At the same time, rising tuition costs were putting education and training out of reach for large numbers of young men and women. Americans in all parts of the country recognized the need to rekindle the spirit of service and community that had helped the nation pull together in earlier times of crisis.

In 1990, Congress passed the National and Community Service Act as a first step in addressing these concerns. Two years later, Bill Clinton made that kind of service an important issue in the presidential campaign. With his leadership, Congress and the Administration worked together to enact the National and Community Service Trust Act of 1993, which built on the foundation laid by the 1990 Act.

The 1993 Act accomplished several goals. First, it funds full-time and part-time service programs around the country. Full-time participants will earn an annual minimum stipend of $7,400 ($6,290 of which will be paid by the federal government) for up to two years of service. They also will receive an educational award of $4,725 for each year served, which they can use to pay for college or vocational school tuition or education loans. Second, the 1993 Act increased funding for "service learning" projects that initially had been funded by the Serve-America program in the 1990 Act; these projects integrate community service activities into the education curriculum, instilling principles of civic responsibility while giving students an opportunity to test new skills through real-life activities. Third, the 1993 Act reauthorized existing domestic service programs such as VISTA. Finally, it created a new Corporation for National and Community Service to administer all federal domestic service programs.

Together, the 1990 Act and the 1993 Act have established a comprehensive national service program that supports service learning projects in the nation's schools, funds successful community service programs across the country, offers citizens the chance to earn vouchers to help pay for education and training, and provides service opportunities for Americans of all ages. By aiding civic organizations and government agencies in their efforts to protect the environment, support education, promote public safety, and reweave the broken strands of the nation's social safety net, these Acts also are helping "servers" and "served" alike to rediscover the ties of community that bind us all together.

I know firsthand how such programs can change lives. As an undergraduate at Harvard University, I took part in service programs organized by a campus volunteer organization at Phillips Brooks House. I worked with a settlement house in one of Boston's poorer neighborhoods, helping to organize recreational activities for children. My most memorable experience from that period was coaching a local youth basketball team. I have now forgotten our won-lost record, but I have not forgotten the sense of teamwork we shared.

Many other members of my family also have been active in founding and supporting service activities. Special Olympics began in the backyard of my sister, Eunice Kennedy Shriver. My sister Jean Kennedy Smith helped to start Very Special Arts, which provides cultural opportunities for people with disabilities. Thanks to the help of many others, both Special Olympics and Very Special Arts have now become international programs that give tens of thousands of people with disabilities the opportunity to participate in sports and the arts, while giving thousands of volunteers the chance to share in their support and their achievements. Today, the next generation of family members is building on these efforts, with programs such as Best Buddies, started by Anthony Shriver to match college students as Big Brothers and Sisters for people with mental retardation; Kathleen Kennedy Townsend's efforts to establish community service activities in the Maryland schools; and the work my son Teddy has done with people who have disabilities.

These activities have shown all of us what a difference service activities can make in the lives of participants. The disabled are not unable. Those who are served gain benefits they might otherwise have had to do without — whether it is the opening of new horizons in sports and the arts, the provision of basic needs like a hot meal and a warm home, or the simple gift of friendship. Those who serve benefit as well by new friends and experiences, by the satisfaction of giving something back to others in return for all they have been given themselves, and by discovering the spirit of kinship and community that transcends any boundaries of race, religion, gender, ethnic background, or social class.

Forerunners of the National and Community Service Trust Act of 1993

The 1960s and early 1970s bequeathed a valuable legacy of service programs to the nation. The best known of these is undoubtedly the Peace Corps. Founded by President Kennedy in 1961, it shares the talents of Americans with other countries across the globe, where volunteers help with projects in areas such as education, health care, agriculture, and economic development. Sargent Shriver was the first director of the Peace Corps, and future Senator Harris Wofford (D-Pa.), who played an important role in shaping the National and Community Service Trust Act of 1993, was one of its first administrators.

On the domestic side, President Johnson established VISTA, which offers small stipends for adults willing to participate full time for a year or more in projects to improve low-income communities. In addition, several volunteer programs for older Americans were established during this period to draw on the experience, skills, and available time of increasing numbers of senior citizens. These Older American Volunteer Programs include the Foster Grandparents Program, which matches senior citizens with at-risk foster children; the Senior Companion Program, which pairs senior citizens who can provide assistance with those requiring help; and the Retired Senior Volunteer Program, which places older Americans in a wide range of community service projects where their experience will be most valuable. Both VISTA and the Older American Volunteer Programs have been administered at the federal level by ACTION, the umbrella agency created by the Domestic Volunteer Service Act of 1973.

In the late 1980s, a number of Senators, including Barbara Mikulski (D-Md.), Christopher Dodd (D-Conn.), Daniel Patrick Moynihan (D-N.Y.), Claiborne Pell (D-R.I.), Sam Nunn (D-Ga.), Dale Bumpers (D-Ark.), and I, began to develop new ideas for national service programs. These included proposals to establish a new federal youth corps and to offer post-service educational awards to participants. I introduced the Serve-America Act to support service learning programs that link community projects with activities in the classroom. In addition, at the grassroots level, communities, civic organizations, and schools were developing new ways for citizens to participate in public service.

In drafting the National and Community Service Act of 1990, we drew on many of these ideas. One section of the Act adopted the Serve-America program, which has fostered the development of partnerships between schools and community organizations across the nation to involve students from kindergarten to grade 12 in service activities. The Act also has offered grants to colleges to create or expand community service programs with educational components. Other sections of the Act authorized competitive grants to states and local organizations to develop pilot projects for youth corps and other programs offering stipends and education or housing benefits in exchange for service. The Act also established a federal Commission on National and Community Service to administer these programs.

The 1990 Act laid a solid foundation for further efforts to develop innovative service programs. Many of its key initiatives — including Serve-America and support for service programs offering educational benefits — provided the model for the National and Community Service Trust Act of 1993.

President Clinton's Leadership

Throughout the 1992 presidential campaign, Bill Clinton stressed the importance of national and community service as a means of instilling the values of citizenship and personal responsibility. President Clinton emphasized this theme in his Inaugural Address in January 1993, when he challenged young Americans to "a season of service" to help in "reconnecting our torn communities." Soon after, an Administration task force began reviewing VISTA, the Older American Volunteer Programs, and the new projects launched by the 1990 Act.

By March 1993, the Administration had distilled its vision into a specific policy. The central element in the President's proposal was a new national service program offering vouchers for education or training in return for a year or more of service. Like the G.I. Bill of an earlier generation, the program would offer educational benefits in return for service to the nation. At the same time, President Clinton also suggested that students borrowing money for education be allowed to repay these loans as a percentage of their income, so that students with large debts could still accept relatively low-paying service jobs. This proposal took shape as the Student Loan Reform Act of 1993, which is discussed elsewhere in this book.

Staff members from the White House Office of National Service began working with the staff of the Senate Labor and Human Resources Committee and the House Education and Labor Committee, and with Senate and House legislative counsel, to draft legislation embodying the President's plan.

The Administration decided to structure its bill as an amendment to the two previous acts that governed most existing service programs — the National and Community Service Act of 1990 and the Domestic Volunteer Service Act of 1973, both of which were due for reauthorization. In taking this approach, the Administration sought to create a coordinated program and ensure continuity with existing federal efforts, rather than simply establish another service program. This approach also enabled the Administration and Congress to incorporate other ideas for strengthening existing programs.

Proposed Legislation

In May 1993, 19 Senators — including four Republicans — and I introduced the Administration's proposal. Our bill was designed to accomplish four objectives. First, it created the National Service Trust Program, providing in-service stipends and post-service education benefits for full-time and part-time participants in selected national and community service programs. Second, it expanded the Serve-America program for service learning. Third, it reauthorized VISTA and the Older American Volunteer Programs. Finally, it created a new administrative structure for all national service programs, integrating them under a new Corporation for National and Community Service, while leaving control over actual service projects in the hands of local grassroots organizations. The legislation was designed to offer a range of opportunities for Americans of all ages: service learning for students, full-time and part-time youth service for those over age 17, and service for older Americans.

Although some had proposed that all student financial aid be conditioned on participation in service programs, the legislation did not impose such a condition. It did not require any person to serve in exchange for federal benefits. Participation by states, communities, and institutions remained entirely voluntary. Like the 1990 Act, the proposal kept federal bureaucracy to a minimum and delegated most decisions about funding to state and local authorities.

Service Learning

The bill's provisions for service learning are of particular importance.* The phrase "service learning" refers to any program that seeks to integrate community service projects into the education curriculum, so that students will have opportunities to test and develop skills and ideas in real-life activities that emphasize the concept of service to others.

Service learning programs can involve students of all ages, from kindergarten to college and beyond. They may be initiated by elementary and secondary schools, by colleges and universities, or by community organizations.

Massachusetts offers countless examples of creative links between service and study. At the Emerson School in Bolton, Massachusetts,

---

*I am concentrating on service learning in this article, since other articles in this volume discuss full-time youth service and service by older Americans.

third- and seventh-graders jointly monitor acquatic life and pollution in a local river. Government regulatory agencies then use this research to determine which waterways need to be cleaned up most urgently. The project enables students to apply their knowledge of ecology and biology, while also helping them to serve the community's environmental goals.

West Roxbury High School students are writing children's books for their elementary school "buddies" and then reading these books with them. The Drumlin Farm Food Project takes Boston students into the country during the summer to plant and tend vegetables; these students later harvest and sell the produce at cost at inner-city farm stands. Their service teaches them about agriculture, biology, nutrition, and basic business.

Even the youngest students can profit from service learning. Eliot Elementary School students in Boston's historic North End are studying the Revolutionary War, retracing the ride of Paul Revere, and becoming guides to teach other elementary school students from nearby communities about that part of our history. These students also plan to serve as guides for the Afro-American Heritage Trail in Boston. Such programs hone students' speaking and writing skills and give them an opportunity to bring history to life.

Service learning is particularly productive when it is incorporated in the curriculum throughout the school system. Boston has moved in this direction by adopting a mandatory service requirement in all of its public high schools. Springfield, Massachusetts, has included service learning since 1987 as part of its school improvement process. In 1993, 135 Springfield teachers were being trained in service learning through a systemwide professional development program. Meanwhile, Springfield students regularly participate in service learning activities at all grade levels.

At Forest Park Middle School in Springfield, a model program trains students as mediators to defuse potentially disruptive school disputes. At the city's Putnam High School, students are planning a low-income community health center that will be located next to the high school. Later, students will staff the center.

Springfield's Putnam High also has been instrumental in two annual citywide Clean-up Days, which have involved students in mapping the downtown merchant area, surveying businesses and youths about trash and recycling, and designing, constructing, and placing outdoor wastebaskets. Through these activities, students have learned about the environment and developed leadership, organizational, and design skills. Students participating in such service learning projects tend to have higher marks (by more than a full grade) and fewer absences (by 50%) than non-participants.

Community groups throughout Massachusetts also have been innovators in combining service and learning. One group, called Facing History and Ourselves, has developed a course using the Holocaust as a historical case study for students to discuss present-day issues of racism and discrimination. Through its "Choosing to Participate" program, Facing History and Ourselves encourages students to intervene against these divisive forces by serving in their communities.

The JFK Library Corps, housed at the John F. Kennedy Library, involves middle school and high school students in community service projects in the Boston area, such as working with HIV-positive children on arts projects.

Another community-based service learning program in Eastern Massachusetts, called Magic Me, has proven especially effective in persuading at-risk youth in schools to assume leadership roles. Magic Me pairs students at six middle schools with senior citizens in nursing homes. The students design programs, such as magic shows, theater performances, oral histories, and dance lessons, for the elderly.

In recent years, I have had the opportunity to visit many of these programs. I have seen the difference that a kindergarten pupil can make in the life of a lonely senior citizen. I have talked to a fifth-grader who helped create a conservation center and learned some basic science at the same time. These and many other experiences demonstrate the value of service learning.

Such programs build an important foundation for citizenship by making service a part of students' lives from a young age. They provide benefits for students, helping them develop leadership qualities and improve academic skills. Studies show that students retain more of the information learned in service projects than in conventional school settings. Schools undertaking such programs report fewer dropouts and more college applicants.

For example, since Keystone Oaks High School in Pennsylvania adopted a mandatory service requirement three years ago, the dropout rate has declined by 75%. At Chestnut Ridge High School in the same state, the percentage of students pursuing postsecondary education rose from 30% to 80% of all students within five years after the school implemented a schoolwide service learning program.

Students involved in school service programs also participate more frequently than control groups in non-school volunteer work, clubs, scouting, and religious activities. Evaluations of students who have served also show that most have a positive impression of service programs and want to serve again. Given these beneficial results, it is not surprising that most major studies on education and youth development in the past decade have advocated service learning as an integral part of school reform. Those who learn the service ethic in their youth are likely to keep it all their lives.

In the 1980s many schools were eager to start or expand service learning programs, but their efforts frequently were limited by the lack of funds. With the passage of the 1990 Act, the Commission on National and Community Service began to support these important programs by funding partnerships between schools, youth organizations, and community agencies. By fiscal year 1992, approximately 275,000 students in kindergarten through grade 12 were involved in service learning programs, at an average cost of only $39 per participant.

The Administration's 1993 bill built upon this foundation by nearly doubling funding to $40 million for fiscal year 1994. It also authorized the use of funds for a number of new activities. For example, the bill allowed federal funding to pay for coordinators to assist individual teachers, schools, and community organizations to plan new service learning projects. The new legislation also increased the percentage of grant funds that could be used for capacity-building activities, such as teacher training. Finally, the bill encouraged grants to universities to help them incorporate service learning into the curriculum for training new teachers.

Administrative Structure

Under the 1993 bill, as under the 1990 Act, the goal was to strengthen schools and community organizations engaged in service projects, not to absorb them into a federal bureaucracy. Those closest to the community know best how to meet local needs. We also wanted to ensure that federal support for community service activities would not jeopardize the creativity that had spawned so many innovative and successful programs. Accordingly, both Acts leave administration of actual service programs essentially under local control. Individuals wishing to participate will be able to obtain lists of programs that have received funding and then apply directly to these programs to be included.

21

There was also a need for greater coordination among all service programs at the federal level. Building on the Commission for National and Community Service established in 1990, the 1993 bill created a new Corporation for National Service to oversee virtually all federal service programs, eventually including VISTA and the Older American Volunteer Programs.

This new corporation will be entrepreneurial in character. Rather than depending solely on government money, it will be authorized to solicit and receive private donations to help fund its efforts. It will be run by a bipartisan citizen board of directors. Corporation employees will not be under a civil service system, but will be covered by a more flexible merit-based personnel system.

At the state level, the Administration's legislation called for the formation of new State Commissions on National Service (or other state agencies approved by the federal corporation). State commissions will be responsible for deciding which local service initiatives to fund, thereby ensuring that the programs respond to local needs. In the case of funding for school-based service learning, funding will be distributed through state education authorities. The competitive process of applying through state commissions will guarantee that high quality programs will be funded; programs across the country will be challenged to devise the most effective and creative uses of the time and energy of participating citizens.

The Committee Process

After introduction in the Senate in May, the Administration's bill was referred to the Senate Committee on Labor and Human Resources, which has jurisdiction over federal education programs. During the next two months, both the full committee and its Subcommittee on Children, chaired by Senator Dodd, held several hearings on the bill to receive comments on the legislation from business and labor leaders, college presidents, state government officials, heads of federal agencies, and community activists. The testimony showed the strong potential of national and community service to improve the lives of participants and those they helped.

Some of the most powerful testimony came from students serving part time — from fourth-graders to college students — as well as from full-time youth corps participants. Cedric Parker, a teenager from Pennsylvania, testified that he had been a high school dropout with few options when he joined the Pennsylvania Conservation Corps. After building a nature center in a state park and assisting in rebuilding houses damaged by Hurricane Andrew, he now has the skills and desire to become a carpenter.

We also heard testimony from senior citizens participating in the Older American Volunteer Programs. Edie Courville, a Senior Companion to Hilda Courbin of Worcester, Massachusetts, testified that her service kept her young and active, despite her 70-plus years of age. And Hilda's daughter testified that Edie's service has inspired her mother and helped to keep her engaged. These kinds of dual benefits illustrate the cost-effectiveness of investing in community service programs.

Based on suggestions received by the Labor and Human Resources Committee, a number of changes were made to the bill. For example, we altered the bill to give state governments an opportunity to explain why priorities developed by the Corporation for National and Community Service should not apply to their state. The bill also was changed to strengthen the role of young men and women on the State Commissions and on the Board of Directors of the corporation.

The committee also adopted a number of suggestions by its members. Senator Jeff Bingaman (D-N.M.) advocated a Public Lands Corps program to undertake historical and cultural preservation on public lands and Indian lands. Senator Howard Metzenbaum (D-Ohio) wanted to allow participants to help convert abandoned military installations into community centers. Senator Paul Wellstone (D-Minn.) sought evaluation of the demographics of those serving and adequate technical assistance to ensure that the program would reach larger numbers of low-income participants. Senator Dodd urged us to extend child-care benefits offered under the new national service trust program to VISTA participants as well. Senator Dave Durenberger (R-Minn.) suggested that the name of the bill and the state commissions and corporation be renamed to emphasize community service as well as national service. Senator Tom Harkin (D-Iowa) worked to ensure that the bill would include individuals with disabilities.

To involve low-income communities effectively, we required that 50% of the national service funding go to programs operating in economically or environmentally distressed areas, with priority for programs recruiting participants from the areas in which they were serving. To allay concerns that federal agencies might apply for funding and crowd out effective local programs, we imposed a 10% ceiling on the percentage of national service funds available for federally run programs.

During this period, the Labor and Human Resources Committee also worked with the Governmental Affairs Committee to ensure proper grant accountability and oversight. We strengthened the corporation's personnel structure, enhanced the accountability provisions, and refined the grant audit provisions.

On 16 June 1993, the Labor and Human Resources Committee reported the bill to the Senate by a vote of 14 to 3. Supporters included all 10 Democratic members of the committee and four Republicans — Senator Durenberger, Senator James Jeffords (R-Vt.), Senator Judd Gregg (R-N.H.), and Senator Dan Coats (R-Ind.). Although Senator Nancy Landon Kassebaum (R-Kans.), the senior Republican member of the committee, opposed the bill, she announced plans to introduce an alternative, because she felt the Administration's bill was too expensive, too bureaucratic, and too prescriptive.

From the perspective of the Administration's supporters, these charges were essentially unfounded. In particular, criticism of the bill's cost was based on faulty analogies and too narrow a calculation of its benefits. Comparisons of national service with other federal education programs, such as Pell grants, overlooked the fact that a significant portion of the cost of national service pays for modest stipends to participants while they serve. Studies of service programs show that the benefits — schools painted, food sorted in food banks, environmental clean-up achieved — are worth approximately twice the cost of these programs. For example, state service corps in Pennsylvania, California, Michigan, and Washington state have calculated direct benefits of $1.70, $1.77, $2.01 and $2.88, respectively, per dollar spent. Beyond these cost-benefit calculations are the unquantifiable but very real benefits that accrue to those who serve — enhanced leadership skills, a lifelong desire to volunteer, and improved chances of landing a paid job after serving.

Critics also tended to focus only on the cost of funding the National Service Trust Program, ignoring other parts of the bill, such as the Serve-America program. The 20,000 National Service Trust Program participants funded in the first year are an important part of the Administration's national service proposal, but their number is small in comparison to the more than one million people whose service will be supported by the bill in its first year through service learning programs and the Older American Volunteer Programs. The estimated federal cost for all participants is far less than the minimum wage per hour served.

Nevertheless, the bill's sponsors wanted to achieve as much bipartisan support as possible without sacrificing essential principles. To address the concerns of some of our colleagues, we discussed a number of possible changes. For example, we worked with Senator Jeffords to ensure that states would develop their own priorities for service needs.

In some cases, however, there were fundamental and unresolvable differences. The argument that the bill was too bureaucratic ignored the organizational simplification it was trying to achieve. It would have been easiest for the Clinton Administration to create a new agency to administer the new program. Instead, to bring existing programs under one roof, the bill consolidated the commission and ACTION into the Corporation for National and Community Service. The legislation gave the corporation the freedom needed to find out how best to integrate these two entities and required a detailed plan for disbursing funds. The Administration's forecast at the time the legislation was adopted was that the corporation could do the task of both entities and oversee the new program with little or no increase in personnel.

There also was fundamental disagreement on other suggestions put forth by opponents. These included reducing educational awards significantly or not offering them to all national service participants, limiting the bill to only two years, and eliminating a number of service programs. A major reduction in the educational award would have impaired its value for opening up new educational opportunities. The program would have been less attractive for low-income participants and would have involved less diversity.

We also were concerned that too much national service funding would be allocated by formula rather than by competition. At a time when many states lacked an adequate infrastructure to support national service programs, excessive "formula funding" would reduce competition for funds and lead to lower quality programs and potentially significant numbers of make-work service positions.

Finally, there were objections that the national service bill would not serve everyone. But the bill was never intended to be universal. There were not enough high quality programs and program leaders nationwide to embark on a universal national service effort without leading to the waste that inevitably results from expanding too quickly.

Senate Consideration

The full Senate began considering the Administration's bill on 20 July 1993. The following day, Senator Kassebaum's substitute version was debated and defeated by a vote of 59 to 38. On July 22, Senator Kassebaum introduced a second substitute amendment, virtually identical to her first. Over the next week, Senator Wofford, Senator Durenberger, and I sought to work out further compromises with Republican Senators to ensure the 60 votes needed under the Senate rules to break any filibuster. Altogether, we were able to reach agreement on enough issues to believe that there was a good chance of winning the votes necessary. We introduced the Kennedy-Durenberger-Wofford substitute bill incorporating these agreements on July 28.

Our substitute reduced the authorization for the program from five years to three years. With respect to costs, we split the difference between the $2.1 billion that the Administration had suggested for its new national service initiative and the $0.9 billion that Senator Kassebaum had proposed for three years of funding. In the end, we agreed on successively greater annual authorizations of $300 million, $500 million, and $700 million over three years. This funding level still provided for 20,000 full-time and part-time stipended national service participants in the first year – more than served in the Peace Corps at its height. Over the three years of the program, the corporation expects to fund a total of 100,000 year-long positions.

We also agreed to a provision, suggested by Senator Durenberger, that would require the corporation to examine some of the fundamental precepts of national service, such as the importance of diversity in programs, the role of educational awards in attracting national service participants, and the administrative structure for the ACTION programs under the corporation. In addition, the substitute included provisions to ensure that participants perform direct service and to limit administrative costs. Clarifying language also was added to prohibit national service participants from lobbying.

In spite of these concessions, some opponents continued to filibuster the bill; and two cloture votes were scheduled to cut off debate. In the initial vote, on July 29, we fell one vote short of the necessary 60 votes. Before the second cloture vote the next day, Republican Leader Bob Dole of Kansas conceded that the opponents no longer had enough votes to maintain their filibuster. The Senate agreed to vote on the bill on August 3.

During debate on July 30, the Senate agreed to five more Republican amendments. One of these modifications reduced the educational benefit for each year of full-time service from $5,000 to $4,725, or 90% of the comparable benefit level under the G.I. Bill. This change addressed the concerns of veterans' groups that the benefits of civilian service should not exceed those for military service. Some service advocates also had favored a lower post-service educational award, believing that a lower benefit would encourage people to sign up because they truly wanted to serve and not simply for the sake of the financial reward.

26

Several other amendments were defeated, including an amendment offered by Senator William Cohen (R-Maine) to "means-test" the post-service educational award and deny it to middle-class participants. The amendment was inconsistent with the principle of national service — that the educational award is earned through service and not based on income. The same principle applies to those who earn education benefits under the G.I. Bill by serving in the armed forces.

An amendment by Senator Arlen Specter (R-Pa.) to reduce the authorization for the bill to two years also was defeated. This shorter time would have made it more difficult to mobilize states to form state commissions on national service because of uncertainty over the bill's reauthorization. Also, a short authorization period would not allow adequate time to assess the program before extending it.

Finally, on August 3, the Senate approved the bill by a vote of 58 to 41, with seven Republicans joining 51 Democrats. The compromises had ended the filibuster, but substantial partisan opposition remained.

Conference and Enactment

The House of Representatives had approved its own version of the Administration's bill on July 28. Even though the Senate and House had begun with identical bills, the legislative process had led to hundreds of differences — many of them minor, but some significant — between the two versions. These differences had to be reconciled in a conference between House and Senate members before the final version could be approved by both chambers.

The Administration and the bill's sponsors worked to hold the conference quickly, in order to complete action before Congress' annual one-month summer recess, which began on August 7. Democratic and Republican staff members in the House and Senate worked rapidly to assess the differences and resolve them. In an effort to avoid a further Senate filibuster, the House-Senate conferees agreed to accept in the same or substantially similar form 26 of the 32 Republican amendments adopted by the Senate, including all of the most significant Republican changes, such as reduced funding levels, the revisions in the structure of the corporation, the studies that Senator Durenberger had directed the corporation to conduct, and the establishment of corporation priorities.

The House approved the conference bill on August 6. But Republican opposition in the Senate remained high, and Senate action could not be completed before the recess began. Undoubtedly, Republican opposition was enhanced by the highly partisan debate and vote on President Clinton's deficit reduction plan, which took place in the Senate on August 6. The final vote on the Act came on September 8, when the conference version was approved by the Senate by a vote of 57 to 40.

President Clinton signed the Act in the Rose Garden at the White House on September 21, in a ceremony that evoked the nation's long-standing tradition of public service. One of the two pens used by President Clinton had been used by President Roosevelt to create the Civilian Conservation Corps in 1933. The other pen had been used by President Kennedy to sign the Peace Corps legislation into law in 1961. Sargent Shriver sat in the front row. Young Americans who had participated in community service programs spoke movingly about their experiences. Eleven-year-old Pricilla Aponte of Boston told how she had worked with her classmates to help the homeless and to plant a garden in an abandoned city lot. The commitment of these young guests was convincing evidence of the importance of harnessing the energy and talents of Americans of all ages for community service.

In its final form as enacted, the new law strengthens existing service programs, such as VISTA and the Older Americans Volunteer Programs; expands the Serve-America service learning program first adopted in 1990; and launches a new program to provide educational benefits in return for full- and part-time youth service. The bill also incorporates innovative concepts, such as a partnership between the public and private sector to fund the program, a private-sector-like corporation to administer it, the allocation of key funding decisions to states and localities, and a non-civil-service hiring system to reduce red tape.

The changes adopted in response to Republican concerns created enough bipartisan support to ensure that the bill would become law. The funding levels are moderate and achievable and will afford steady, but prudent growth. The lower funding levels also will increase competition among service programs, so that only the best will receive federal money. Senator Jeffords' suggestion directing the states and the corporation to develop priorities ensures that these programs will meet vital community needs.

Service and America's Future

National and community service is one of the best investments our nation can make. It will attack vexing federal, state, and local problems, such as homelessness, pollution, crime, and illiteracy. At the same time, it will instill virtues of caring, responsibility, and citizenship in those who serve. By making Americans better citizens, we improve America, too.

Students who would otherwise drop out can be motivated to stay in school through involvement in service. Others will be inspired to pursue careers in public service or to develop career goals linking service with work. Those who serve will gain valuable experience and leadership skills that not only will make it easier to find paid employment, but will make them more active citizens in our democracy. They also will serve as role models and inspire others to make a difference themselves.

America needs to recapture the sense of community that has provided the foundation for the nation's success in the past. Enactment of this national and community service legislation stands as a defining moment of this Congress and President Clinton's Administration. Investments in community service today and in the coming years will bring substantial benefits to the country.

In his 1961 Inaugural Address, President Kennedy touched a deeply responsive chord when, in his famous phrase, he urged us to ask what we could do for our country. Recently, I met with some of the first volunteers in the Peace Corps. I asked them, "Why did you do it? How did you come to be a part of this new program, with so many risks and so little compensation?" Their response, eloquent in its insight, was, "No one ever asked us before."

With the passage of the National and Community Service Trust Act of 1993, we are asking again. We are challenging Americans to reach out to others and to rediscover the strengths of personal responsibility, community involvement, and national purpose that have made this nation great, and that will keep it great in the future.

National Service: A Watchful Concern

By Senator Nancy Landon Kassebaum

Nancy Landon Kassebaum of Kansas was elected to the United States Senate in 1978. Now serving her third term, she is the ranking Republican member of the Senate Committee on Labor and Human Resources. The Labor Committee has legislative jurisdiction over a broad range of domestic programs — including all programs administered by the Departments of Education and Labor as well as a number of health and children's programs administered by the Department of Health and Human Services.

Senator Kassebaum also serves on the Committee on Foreign Relations, the Committee on Indian Affairs, and the Joint Committee on the Organization of Congress. She has a B.A. in political science from the University of Kansas and an M.A. in diplomatic history from the University of Michigan and is the mother of four children.

The seeds of the idea that took shape as the National and Community Service Trust Act of 1993 were planted during the Bush-Clinton presidential campaign of 1992. Although it was never a dominant issue in the campaign, national service was a theme which then-candidate Clinton voiced repeatedly on the stump and echoed in his victory speech on the evening of November 3 and in his Inaugural Address on January 20. The "100th day" of the Clinton Presidency — April 30 — was marked by a major national service speech in New Orleans as a prelude to the introduction of legislation one week later.

Just a few weeks prior to Clinton's taking the oath of office, I assumed the position of ranking Republican member of the Senate Committee on Labor and Human Resources. The Labor Committee has legislative jurisdiction over a broad range of domestic programs. Any national service bill would be referred to the Labor Committee upon introduction.

31

Given the President's frequent mention of the subject, it was clear from the outset that a national service bill would be introduced. Moreover, the chairman of the committee, Senator Ted Kennedy, had been an enthusiastic proponent of national service programs. I took this into account in anticipating what the committee's agenda might be during the 103rd Congress.

The First 100 Days

Although it was clear that national service legislation would be on the agenda, it was not at all clear what shape that legislation would take. The concept was painted in very broad strokes during the campaign.

Typical of the discussion was the description of the idea included in *Putting People First*:

> [S]crap the existing student loan program, and establish a National Service Trust Fund to guarantee every American who wants a college education the means to obtain one. Those who borrow from the fund will pay it back either as a small percentage of their income over time, or through community service as teachers, law enforcement officers, health care workers, or peer counselors helping kids stay off drugs and in school.

Congressional Republicans were not involved in the process of putting a specific proposal together (nor did we expect to be). As an observer during the "first 100 days" as the Administration's proposal was put together, I saw three main challenges that the Administration would face in developing and selling a bill.

First, the concepts put forward by the President were broad enough to give encouragement to proponents of several competing service models. One of the first tasks had to be determining what direction the legislation should go.

During those early days, it appeared to me that a healthy debate was under way with respect to the model the bill should follow. Some preferred a structured program along the lines of the Peace Corps or youth service corps, where those engaged in a period of full-time service would receive forgiveness of college loans. Others argued on behalf of loan forgiveness for individuals who entered service professions, such as those described in *Putting People First*, whether or not they were part of a structured program.

Added to the difference of opinion about the appropriate "service" model were the voices of those who preferred equal or greater emphasis on "volunteerism" models, which are generally part-time rather than full-time. These include service learning programs at the elementary and secondary levels, precollege service opportunities where individuals can build credit for college aid, and programs involving non-college-bound young people or older Americans.

A second challenge was devising a program that would stay within the confines of a realistic federal budget. Taken literally, the ideas put forward by the President would have had a price tag of tens of billions of dollars each year.

For example, at one point, the President spoke of offering $10,000 in loan forgiveness to any student who spent one year in full-time service. If even 5% of the nation's 15 million college students had taken advantage of such an offer, the first-year cost for the education benefits alone would have been $7.5 billion — an amount five times greater than the three-year cost of the bill eventually signed into law.

Finally, a good deal of confusion and complexity was injected into the debate because the President linked the concepts of national service, direct student loans, and income-contingent loan repayment. The linkage of these issues not only created practical problems in terms of moving a bill through the legislative process, but also threatened a loss of support from a fairly substantial number of members who favored national service but had grave reservations about direct lending. For example, the enthusiasm for national service of members such as Senators Claiborne Pell, Sam Nunn, and Jim Jeffords was perhaps matched by their skepticism about direct lending.

The practical problem with the linkage was that consideration of changes to entitlement programs, such as the guaranteed student loan program, was made as part of the budget reconciliation process. Under what is known as the "Byrd rule," discretionary spending programs — those with funding levels subject to annual appropriations — may not be included in a budget reconciliation bill. National service is a discretionary spending program.

Preview of Program and Initial Reaction

My first exposure to the specifics of the legislation being prepared by the Administration came in the form of an April 23 letter confirming a meeting with Eli Segal, Assistant to the President and Director of National Service. The letter was accompanied by a nine-page summary of the proposal.

The April 27 meeting with Mr. Segal was the first of many that I and my staff had with him over the course of the next five months.

Mr. Segal was spearheading the Administration's national service effort. Ray Chambers of the Points of Light Foundation; Nick Lowery, player on the Kansas City Chiefs football team; and Jack Lew, legal counsel in the White House Office of National Service, accompanied Mr. Segal to the meeting. Also joining the meeting were two members of my Labor Committee staff: Susan Hattan, minority staff director, and Kimberly Barnes-O'Connor, minority children's policy coordinator, whom I had asked to take the lead in staffing the national service issue.

During the first part of the meeting, Mr. Segal, Mr. Chambers, and Mr. Lowry talked about their commitment to the concept of national service and expressed their interest in obtaining bipartisan support for the President's initiative.

I turned the conversation to the student loan piece of the proposal, as I had noted that it was highlighted on the first page of the summary sent to me by Mr. Segal. At the time, I was focused particularly on the direct lending component because initial congressional action to implement it already had taken place as part of the budget process. During Senate consideration of the budget resolution in March, I had offered an amendment designed to ensure that the Labor Committee would have options other than adoption of a full-scale direct lending program in meeting the budget savings required by the resolution. I believed that budget savings attributed to direct lending were illusory. I also was concerned about the impact of the proposal on increasing federal debt and about the ability of the Department of Education to manage the program.

I strongly urged Mr. Segal to separate the direct student loan proposal from the national service initiative, rather than to combine them in a single bill. I pointed out that the linkage of the two issues was confusing and detracted from the ability of members to debate the merits of either proposal.

The following day, Administration officials met with several Republican Senate staffers to present additional information about the national service proposal. It was announced at that meeting that the national service and direct loan proposals would be submitted as separate pieces of legislation.

A fairly clear picture emerged from that meeting about how the Administration envisioned the national service program operating. A new federal corporation would be created to administer the program. The cost of the program was estimated to be $400 million in fiscal year 1994, growing to $3.4 billion by 1997 — for a total cost of $7.4 billion over the measure's four-year authorization period.

Beginning with 25,000 participants in the first year, the program was expected to expand to include 100,000 to 150,000 national service participants during the fourth year of operation. Service learning and part-time community volunteer programs also were included in the package.

Administration officials stated that the national service program would be locally driven and flexible enough to respond to the unique needs of American communities. They envisioned very broad national eligibility criteria to allow maximum diversity in the types of local programs that would be funded and the characteristics of the participants in national service.

Educational benefits, amounting to $6,500 for each year of service, could be used to pay off student loans or to finance current or future postsecondary education expenses. The program would not be means-tested, thereby encouraging diversity among participants.

Over the next several days, I reviewed the outline of the initiative and considered my response to it. My initial impulse was simply to oppose the measure.

This impulse had its basis in my skepticism about the ability of government programs to foster widespread commitment to lifelong service to one's community. I have long believed that service activities should be based in the community and that financial reward should not be seen as the incentive for offering service. True service is that which is freely given because one wants to make a real difference in improving the quality of community life. It should not be regarded as an obligation to be met for a year or two and then abandoned.

To me, the concept of community-based volunteerism is the most important aspect of service. This is not to deny the value of the full-time service options offered by organizations such as the Peace Corps and VISTA for those individuals who wish to pursue them. It is simply to say that the impact of such programs is inherently limited, whereas cultivation of a sense of individual responsibility to be of service to others is something that can make a difference in each and every community in our nation. We in Washington have the power to pass costly programs and launch national initiatives, but we are totally powerless to create those caring, committed individuals on whom every success depends.

It was for these reasons, in fact, that I did oppose the National and Community Service Act of 1990.

Ultimately, I decided against outright rejection of a national service initiative. I came to this decision, in part, because the 1990 legislation

35

had produced more positive results than I had expected of it and had done so without amassing a gigantic administrative staff in Washington. I also thought that some aspects of the proposal offered a real opportunity to consolidate national service efforts. I concluded that the best chance to help ensure that the new program would be manageable in scope and rational in design was to work on behalf of changes in the proposal.

Introduction of S. 919

Because I had received a number of inquiries from the press and other members of the Senate about my initial reactions to the national service initiative, I decided to make some remarks on the Senate floor about it.

I arrived on the floor the afternoon of May 6, statement in hand, to find Senator Ted Kennedy and several proponents of the measure getting ready to introduce it. I delivered my remarks, feeling rather like "the skunk at the picnic."

In that statement, I lauded the President for his commitment to service and for building the new program on the foundation of existing entities, rather than adding something entirely new. At the same time, I raised concerns about the size of the program, the rapid rate of expansion anticipated for it, the wisdom of this approach as a means of providing educational benefits at a time when existing means-tested programs were not sufficiently funded, and its ability to achieve its intended effect of cultivating a lifelong commitment to service.

As introduced, the National and Community Service Trust Act of 1993 (S. 919) was 263 pages long. In general, it followed along the lines described in the April 28 staff briefing. One significant change was a reduction in the size of the educational award for each year of service, from $6,500 to $5,000. This revision was made in response to concerns that the program offered more generous education benefits than are provided under the GI Bill.

My staff began a more detailed review of its provisions and also initiated research into existing national service and domestic volunteer programs. In the meantime, the legislation was put on a "fast track" in the Labor Committee with hearings scheduled to begin on May 11.

Choosing a Course of Action

As I learned more about the specifics of the legislation, I grew increasingly concerned about it. The initial fears I had expressed were borne out by the details of the bill. Moreover, on closer examination, what had initially appeared to be a true melding of some existing programs turned out, instead, to be a bureaucratic superstructure on top of them.

The question for me at that point became one of determining how best to try to move the bill in a more positive direction. My basic options were either to develop a series of amendments to the bill or to develop a substitute proposal.

The amendment option offered the advantages of requiring fewer staff resources and less time to develop. Given the speed at which S. 919 appeared to be going through the committee process, time was of the essence. The substitute route, on the other hand, offered the advantage of being able to put forward my ideas in a more complete and coherent fashion.

Following discussions with my staff, I concluded that there were a number of serious problems with the structure of S. 919, that my ideas would be more effectively presented in a substitute proposal than in a series of amendments, and that drafting a substitute was feasible even in a compressed time frame.

Concerns with S. 919 and Proposed Solutions

Several concepts — program consolidation, streamlined administration, state flexibility, fiscal restraint, and reasonable growth rates — provided the foundation for the construction of my alternative to the National Service Trust Act. A number of issues emerged as the legislation was crafted, but these concepts guided the decisions that were made throughout the process.

For many reasons, I believed that alternative approaches were preferable to those outlined in S. 919 in terms of meeting these objectives.

Rate of expansion and cost of the program. In January 1993, the staff of the Commission on National and Community Service issued a study of the expansion of national service programs, titled *Growth and Cost Scenario for National Service.* The study represented a thoughtful and thorough examination of the potential for expanding national service programs. The study presented a three-year development plan for a national service network, requiring a "dramatic growth rate, averaging about 50% annually."

The commission estimated that it would be possible to double the current level of 30,000 full-time national service participants in one year's time. By adding approximately 20,000 new participants each year, they concluded that 100,000 individuals could be accommodated in meaningful full-time service opportunities by the end of year three.

To make the projections, the commission's study presupposed folding in and building on many existing federal programs, including work-study, some elements of the Jobs Training Partnership Act (JTPA), the Peace Corps, the National Health Service Corps, and welfare transition programs.

In contrast, the proposed legislation envisioned an even more dramatic rate of growth but did not attempt to incorporate these existing programs into the national service program or to link them in any meaningful way.

I was very concerned about the rate of expansion proposed by the Administration's bill and questioned how national service could absorb a ten-fold increase over four years and maintain the quality that exemplified the existing commission programs.

Another troubling difference between the expansion study and the Administration's proposal involved the cost of the program. In the study, the additional program cost for an expansion of national service to include 100,000 participants was calculated to be $1.6 billion (or $2.1 billion if nonfederal costs were included). The Administration projected a federal cost of $3.4 billion by the fourth year for the same number of participants envisioned in its proposal.

In comparing the two documents I realized that, if some or all of the strategies identified in the commission study could be implemented, the cost of national service would be significantly reduced.

Bureaucratic Structure. A related issue was the bureaucratic structure being proposed in the legislation. The bill placed a few existing national service programs, the ACTION agency, and service-learning programs under the jurisdiction of a new Corporation for National Service. However, the legislation went to great pains to ensure that each of these programs would continue to operate as separate entities within the structure of the corporation.

In my view, the massive expansion of national service and the President's interest in "reinventing government" provided an excellent opportunity for restructuring these programs to make them more responsive to community needs. This would require a true transformation of these programs and their administrative structures, rather than imposing an umbrella-type superstructure on top of the existing agencies.

It seemed to me that the best way to address this concern would be to fold more of the existing national service and domestic volunteer services into the new Corporation for National Service. The structure I envisioned would transform all appropriate existing national service programs into a single full-time national service program offering uniform benefits and service commitments. Likewise, domestic volunteer service programs — those that entail part-time commitments — would be blended.

The advantages of such an approach would be the elimination of competition among federal programs for scarce discretionary dollars and a decrease in overall administrative costs at the state and federal levels. Individual program appropriations for existing programs would be subsumed into the overall budget of the corporation, rather than maintaining separate budgets and requirements for narrowly defined categorical programs.

State Flexibility. The Administration claimed to provide a great deal of local autonomy and flexibility in operating the national service program. However, the prescriptiveness of the legislation combined with the administrative structure and the distribution of funds clearly placed primary control over the program with the federal government.

To address these concerns, I determined that a greater share of the funds available under the bill should be under the control of the states to be allocated under a state plan, rather than a national plan, and that a number of other federal requirements should be eliminated.

Provision of Educational Benefits. Another major concern that the legislation presented involved the use of limited educational dollars for the post-service benefits to be provided to national service participants. At the time the bill was introduced, Congress and the Administration were struggling with significant funding shortfalls in the Pell grant program. In addition, the Administration had recommended dramatic cutbacks in campus-based educational assistance programs, such as work-study.

There was little research on the optimum level of post-service benefits or on the impact of those benefits with respect to the recruitment or the quality of participants in national service-type programs. For example, VISTA provides an unrestricted post-service benefit of less than $1,200. Other existing national service programs provide a broad variety of post-service benefits.

With the limited amount of knowledge and resources available, I thought a more reasonable approach would be to establish demonstration programs to determine what educational or other post-service benefits are necessary for successful national service programs and to identify the best model for incorporating them into the federal effort.

Drafting the Alternative

The drafting process entailed the full-time effort of three staff people: Kimberly Barnes-O'Connor, Carla Widener, and Mary Elizabeth Larson. The process began in earnest in late May with the identification of the major problem areas in S. 919 and proposed solutions to them and the development of an outline of my alternative.

At that time, Eli Segal was advised of my decision to introduce an alternative bill. The basic outline of my alternative proposal was provided to him, as well as to the staffs of Senators Kennedy and Wofford. Based on that outline, my staff met with Administration officials and the Kennedy and Wofford staffs to determine whether there was any common ground on which a compromise effort could be forged. Unfortunately, the differences in approach were too extensive to be resolved by the compromise effort.

My staff began an all-out effort to draft the legislation in the first week of June. There were several drafting options available; and after meeting with legislative counsel, we determined that it would be easier for everyone involved to use S. 919 as a guide. This would facilitate comparing the two pieces of legislation, because section numbers and legislative provisions would be in roughly the same place in each bill. The disadvantage to this approach was that S. 919, apparently having been put together in some haste, was poorly organized.

For the next three and a half weeks, the three-person national service team on my staff dedicated their full time and energies to constructing the legislation. They began referring to it as "the bill that never ends," as they devoted nights and weekends to writing and refining the language, considering options, and overcoming drafting obstacles.

Senate Committee on Labor and Human Resources Markup

Prior to the markup of S. 919, staff of members of the committee met to discuss their concerns and make recommendations, most of which involved relatively minor technical changes, the inclusion of clarifying language, or the addition of specific program initiatives. That discussion formed the basis for more than 10 pages of modifications to the legislation, which were presented at the markup by Senator Kennedy.

The Senate Committee on Labor and Human Resources marked up S. 919 on June 16, after postponing the original markup scheduled for June 9. Although I had hoped to present my legislation at that time, my staff and legislative counsel were still putting the finishing touches on the bill. I restated my concerns about the legislation and informed my colleagues that I soon would be introducing an alternative bill.

I was extremely disappointed that it did not prove possible to complete the drafting of my substitute in time to present it in committee. Although my proposal was shorter than the 260-plus pages of S. 919, it still represented a massive undertaking.

During the markup, Senator Dave Durenberger remarked that he had gone back to look at the legislation that created the Civilian Conservation Corps during the New Deal era. As I recall, he found that it ran about three and a half pages long. It struck me at the time that this contrast said a lot about what had happened in the legislative process and in government in general during those intervening years. Even my proposal, with its objectives of consolidating programs and streamlining bureaucracy, ended up being just under 200 pages in length.

The committee reported the bill to the full Senate by a vote of 14 to 3. Along with Senators Thurmond and Hatch, I submitted minority views to the report on the bill, which was filed on June 29.

Introducing S. 1212: The Kassebaum Alternative

In preparation for introduction of my substitute bill, I circulated a "Dear Colleague" letter to the other members of the Senate. This letter explained my concerns about S. 919, offered a brief description of my alternative, and solicited support for it. A three-page summary of the major provisions of the legislation accompanied the letter.

Hoping to obtain bipartisan support for the legislation if at all possible, I personally handed the material to several Democratic senators whom I believed might be interested in the approach I was taking. In the meantime, my staff called the offices of all the senators who were not co-sponsoring S. 919 and prepared a side-by-side comparison of the two bills. During this time, staff in several offices requested additional information about the proposal and asked questions about specific provisions.

My first opportunity to discuss publicly the details of my alternative came on June 24 at a national service forum sponsored by the House and Senate Republican leadership and attended by several members of both bodies. Attendees included both proponents and opponents of the Administration's national service bill. Proponents put forward reasons they believed the measure merited Republican support, while several House members discussed amendments they were promoting.

I distributed a detailed summary of my proposed national service alternative. I also presented a chart showing the flow of federal funds as proposed by S. 919 and one showing the flow of funds under my proposal. These charts highlighted the cumbersome and complex structure being proposed by the Administration.

The forum offered me a valuable "test run" of my proposal. I remember particularly the reaction to my charts of one of the proponents of S. 919, who remarked, "Well, Nancy. It's just that you make bigger boxes!" I realized that I had my work cut out for me in terms of getting my colleagues to understand that I was truly trying to create one program through consolidation, not merely to maintain separate programs under a single umbrella.

I introduced the "National Service and Community Volunteers Act of 1993," S. 1212, on July 1. Senators Cochran, Hatfield, Stevens, and Thurmond joined with me as original co-sponsors.

My introductory statement delineated the problems I saw with S. 919 and the objectives that I hoped to achieve in my bill:

> My concerns about the President's national service proposal can be summarized succinctly: It is too costly, too bureaucratic, and too prescriptive.
>
> In terms of cost, initial estimates indicate that national service spending will amount to $7.4 billion over four years. This is not only a large amount in and of itself, but it also represents an unwise rate of expansion in national service efforts.
>
> In terms of bureaucracy, on first glance, it appears that the Clinton proposal builds upon the existing foundations of the ACTION agency and the Commission on National Service. Upon closer examination, however, one finds that the proposal actually creates a new superstructure – the Corporation for National Service – under which these existing entities will operate. State ACTION offices will continue to operate side-by-side with state commissions on national service.
>
> In terms of prescriptiveness, the bill takes a top-down approach which threatens to overpower locally based initiatives with federal mandates. Among other things, S. 919 requires that state plans reflect nationally designed – not state-specific – priorities. It dictates the membership of state service commissions, including a requirement that a federal employee of the Corporation serve as a voting member of each state commission. In addition, it goes so far as to prescribe not only state applications for federal funds but also the application and award procedures for state grants to local communities.

I believe there is an opportunity to develop a more rational and streamlined approach which avoids the problems I have identified with S. 919. The legislation I am proposing is intended to meet the following objectives:

1. True integration of federal service efforts in a single, consolidated program.
2. Maximum state flexibility to determine needs and priorities.
3. Recognition of legitimate fiscal constraints and the need for a rate of expansion which is reasonable.
4. Experimentation with post-service benefit concepts prior to undertaking a full-scale commitment to a $5,000 educational benefit.

First, my proposal provides for a two-year transition period during which most existing full-time national service and part-time federally funded volunteer programs would be incorporated into a single federal entity. The new program would provide a consistent set of stipends and benefits, while allowing maximum latitude for states and localities to develop the programs which best fit their needs.

Second, the proposal would require that funds be allocated to local entities based on individual state plans — not on a single national plan. Rather than retaining two-thirds of the funding for allocation by the federal government, as S. 919 does, my proposal will provide 75 percent of volunteer funds, 50 percent of national service funds, and 90 percent of service learning funds directly to the states for distribution.

Third, new first-year spending under my proposal will be approximately $100 million, compared to the nearly $400 million authorized under S. 919. This amount would permit approximately 5,000 new full-time national service positions in addition to the 20,000 such positions supported by the existing programs that are incorporated in my legislation. I believe this rate of expansion is far more realistic than the 25,000 new positions (vs. the 5,000 new positions in my bill) anticipated under S. 919.

Finally, my proposal calls for an 18-month demonstration program to determine the most reasonable level of post-service benefits for a successful national service program and the most efficient method for providing those benefits. Funding for the demonstration would be authorized at $10 million in the first year and $20 million in the second.

It just seems to me that S. 919 is an initiative with enormous potential to grow out of hand, spawning new bureaucracies, new regulations, and make-work positions. It would be a mistake to approve it in its present form. The alternative I am proposing attempts to design a federal role in national service which will pull things together in a rational, efficient administrative structure and implement initiatives at a measured pace. I urge my colleagues to join with me in this effort.

Senate Floor Debate

The early weeks of July following the introduction of S. 1212 were spent preparing for Senate floor debate on national service. Realizing that there was little likelihood that my substitute legislation would be approved by the Senate, my staff began preparing amendments to S. 919. These amendments, while not focused on the massive structural changes envisioned in the substitute, proposed changes to specific provisions that were viewed as problematic. Other Republicans contacted me and my staff to indicate that they had amendments as well.

On July 18, at the request of Eli Segal, I met with him, Shirley Sagawa, and other staff members from the Office of National Service to discuss the pending action on the national service bill. In that meeting I identified my two primary problems with the Administration proposal: the rate of expansion and the administrative structure. They were unable to make any significant movement on either of these issues, and so we basically agreed to disagree.

By July 20 there was a list of 53 possible Republican amendments to S. 919, including those identified by my staff. My staff met with Senator Kennedy's staff in an attempt to negotiate acceptance of some of these amendments. These discussions focused primarily on relatively noncontroversial amendments related to eliminating some of the prescriptiveness in the bill. It was agreed that 10 of these amendments would be accepted during the floor debate on the bill.

The Senate began the floor debate on the "National and Community Service Trust Act," S. 919, on July 20. On the other side of the Capitol, the House of Representatives was debating H.R. 2010, the companion bill to S. 919.

As is common practice in the Senate, the first day of debate was devoted to general discussion of the bill. I took the opportunity with my opening statement not only to reiterate the concerns that prompted my development of a substitute but also to attempt to clarify some public misperceptions about the provisions of S. 919. Specifically, I pointed out that the bill allowed a few, but not all, college students to work off their loans by performing national service and that participants would be paid for their service, unlike the thousands who at the time were volunteering their help with Midwest flood relief efforts.

My substitute, which incorporated the provisions of S. 1212, was the first amendment offered during the second day of floor consideration. Following two hours of debate, the amendment was defeated by a vote of 38 to 59.

The main objections to my amendment came from senators who supported general educational awards as part of the program and those who believed that existing programs such as VISTA and Foster Grandparents should be maintained in their present form, rather than having their functions be part of a consolidated program. In addition, the fact that S. 919 was an initiative of President Clinton had a powerful influence on Democratic members of the Senate, only one of whom supported my amendment.

During this second day of floor debate, most of the action on the bill took place off the floor of the Senate. The most significant development was that an increasing number of Republicans became focused on the national service legislation, and a substantial ground swell of opposition to it developed. A special meeting of the Republican Conference called to discuss the bill brought many members to their feet to express concerns about the bill, while only two of the four Republican co-sponsors of the measure spoke on its behalf.

Given the relative calm that had surrounded the national service issue prior to this time, the intensity of the opposition that was developing had not been expected. Two things help explain why opposition built.

First, members of the Senate generally focus on issues under consideration by the committees on which they serve, giving relatively less attention to other issues until they are debated on the floor. Two days of floor debate on S. 919 brought national service issues into focus, and many members simply did not like what they saw.

Second, it is important to remember that this debate was taking place while members were in the midst of negotiating the final provisions of a budget reconciliation bill calling for increased energy taxes and spending reductions in such programs as Medicare and Medicaid. Preoccupation with budget issues brought to the forefront the question of whether this was the time to be committing more than $7 billion for the creation of a new federal program.

The broad-based reaction led to a shift in the dynamics of the debate. It became possible, through a united front, to obtain significant changes in the legislation that would not otherwise have been achieved. The primary Republican objectives became: 1) reducing the level of funding authorized for the program and 2) shortening the length of the authorization period.

As reported from committee, S. 919 provided for a four-year authorization period with a funding level of $400 million in fiscal year 1994 and "such sums as may be necessary" in the three subsequent years. Although the "such sums" figures were not specified, the President's budget included cost estimates showing that the annual cost of the program would reach $3.4 billion during the fourth year of operation.

On the third day of debate, 14 amendments were accepted to the bill without debate, while two others were rejected by roll call votes. One of the amendments that was defeated, offered by Senator Domenici, would have required full funding of the Pell grant shortfall and funding of campus-based programs at fiscal year 1993 levels prior to the provision of educational benefits under the national service program.

At this point, Senator Helms offered an unrelated amendment extending the patent of the United Daughters of the Confederacy. This amendment, rejected in the Judiciary Committee, largely through the efforts of Senator Moseley-Braun, began an hours-long debate culminating in the rejection of the amendment. Unlike the House, Senate rules do not preclude the offering of nongermane amendments.

Late in the day, I offered my second substitute amendment. The only significant changes from my original amendment concerned the level and duration of the bill's authorization — a two-year authorization funded at $100 million for each year. The Senate rejected the amendment by a vote of 43 to 57.

This vote made it clear to Democratic senators that the bill was facing substantially more opposition than originally anticipated and that Republicans could delay the passage of the legislation. As a result, Senator Mitchell filed a cloture petition — the first step in a process to limit further debate on S. 919. The cloture vote was scheduled to take place on Tuesday, July 27, and negotiations between the two sides would continue during this time.

Again, the action moved off the floor of the Senate, with extensive negotiations occurring on the remaining amendments and on the funding level and number of years to be authorized in the legislation. Senator Dole also was engaged in discussions with Administration officials. In addition, Senators Durenberger and Kennedy were working to craft a substitute amendment addressing many of the concerns raised on and off the floor by Republican and Democratic members.

On July 27 negotiations on the authorization levels appeared promising, and the cloture vote was vitiated. The next day, the Kennedy-Durenberger substitute amendment was introduced, and all other unresolved amendments to the bill were filed. Two cloture petitions were then filed on the Kennedy-Durenberger substitute. The first cloture vote was scheduled for July 29 and the second for Friday, July 30.

The House passed H.R. 2010 on July 28. The next day, the Senate failed to agree to cloture by a vote of 59 to 41, one vote short of the 60 required to limit debate. Although most Republicans knew that the second cloture vote would receive the required 60 votes, the Democrats appeared uncertain; and negotiations on the bill's authorization levels resumed.

The next morning, Senator Cohen announced that he would not vote against cloture on the second roll call vote. Knowing that the cloture vote was now unnecessary, the Senate moved directly to consideration of the Durenberger-Kennedy compromise proposal. This amendment contained a three-year authorization with funding set at $300 million for the first year, $500 million for the second, and $700 million for the third. It also included provisions requiring a review of the administrative structure of the national service program and provisions designed to facilitate congressional oversight as the program grew.

The vote on final passage of the bill was scheduled for the following Tuesday, August 3. Thus, after the addition of some 30 amendments and 14 roll call votes, the legislation was adopted by a vote of 58 to 41. The Senate immediately requested a conference with the House and appointed conferees.

Conference

The conference process began with meetings between House and Senate Democratic staff and Administration officials prior to Senate approval of S. 919. More formal staff negotiations began the evening of August 4 and resumed the next morning. In all, less than 12 hours were spent negotiating the final legislation. Conferees met briefly on the afternoon of August 5 to approve the report, which retained the funding levels and three-year authorization period included in the Senate version of the bill.

The House approved the bill the following afternoon. Senator Kennedy wanted the Senate to pass the conference report that day as well. Because several members requested a roll call vote with some time for debate, efforts to reach a time agreement for consideration were undertaken. Before an agreement could be reached, the Senate approved the budget reconciliation bill; and Senator Mitchell announced that there would be no more roll call votes that evening. Since the Senate was adjourning for the August recess that night, this meant that the national service legislation could not be passed before September if a roll call vote was necessary.

An attempt by Senator Kennedy to pass the bill by voice vote generated several emotional exchanges among members. As the debate continued, I went to the floor to express my concerns about the haste with which the final bill was drafted and to note that errors in the conference documents were creating great confusion among members.

Ultimately, Senator Kennedy withdrew his request after obtaining an agreement that debate on the national service conference report would take place immediately after Senate consideration of the Joycelyn Elders nomination.

On September 8, the Senate passed, by a vote of 57 to 40, the National and Community Service Trust Act of 1993. Once again, I voted against the measure.

President Clinton signed the bill into law on 21 September 1993.

Looking Ahead

The new Corporation for National and Community Service is up and running, having received the full $300 million authorized for its activities in fiscal year 1994. Eli Segal was confirmed by the Senate as chief executive officer of the corporation in October.

I am disappointed that we did not take the opportunity offered by the establishment of this new program to pull together national service efforts, but I have not lost hope that this concept will enjoy greater appeal in the future.

It seems to me that a certain amount of competition is likely to arise between state ACTION offices and state commissions on national and community service. There may be competition as well among the various federal agencies administering similar service programs in terms of attracting participants and obtaining service slots. Depending on how this situation develops, there may well be sentiment for reducing duplication of effort and offering greater uniformity in pay and benefit packages.

I remain concerned as well about the projected rate of expansion of the effort and will be watching carefully to ensure that the quality of service placements is not sacrificed as the program grows.

Having said that, I would note that a powerful force working in favor of the ultimate success of the effort is the commitment to it of individuals such as Eli Segal. In the many conversations we had throughout the year, I was struck consistently by the sincerity and determination he and his staff brought to the effort. As I have often observed, it is not so much programs, but rather people, that make the difference.

An Independent Sector Perspective on National and Community Service

By Roger Landrum

Roger Landrum is president of Youth Service America. Since serving as a Peace Corps volunteer in the early 1960s in Nigeria, Dr. Landrum has worked tirelessly to build a basis in reality for the ideal of national youth service. He founded and directed the nation's first private urban teacher corps, The Teachers Inc. And he directed the Potomac Institute's Committee for the Study of National Service, which published an influential 1979 report, Youth and the Needs of the Nation.

Dr. Landrum has been an advisor on national service to foundations, Capitol Hill, and young entrepreneurs. He chaired or co-chaired the Working Group on Youth Service Policy and the Coalition for National and Community Service. He has published extensively on the subject of national service and appeared on "Nightline" and the "MacNeil/Lehrer News Hour."

Dr. Landrum has a doctoral degree from Harvard University. He has taught at Harvard, Yale, and the University of Nigeria. He recently received the Distinguished Alumnus Award from his alma mater, Albion College.

Only a decade ago, it seemed improbable that by 1993 national service would be so high on the nation's agenda. During the 1970s and 1980s, occasional national service bills introduced by members of the Congress seldom made their way out of committee. An American Conservation Corps Act narrowly passed Congress in 1984 but died with a presidential veto. In a 1986 book, *National Service: What Would It Mean?* Richard Danzig and Peter Szanton called national service, "not an idea, still less a plan, but rather an ideal encompassing a variety of often inconsistent ideas." An old American tradition of volunteerism remained a vital part of American society, but most proponents of domestic national service envisioned a large-scale federal program. Such a program lacked a significant political or grassroots constituency.

Yet today national service is a centerpiece of the presidency of Bill Clinton. Within three years, the National and Community Service Act of 1990 and the National and Community Service Trust Act of 1993 have been enacted by Congress and signed into law by a Republican and a Democratic President, respectively. Innovative programs have been spreading across the country for a decade; and with a new infusion of federal funds and presidential leadership, the pace of expansion will quicken. A substantial constituency for national service both within government and outside has taken shape. What accounts for this transformation? And will the swift rise of national service become a sustained success?

Many Americans share the impression that the origins of the 1993 legislation are to be found in the 1992 election platform of President Clinton. Others assume that the progress of national and community service will be shaped by the new federal agency and state commissions being created by the legislation. But the real story behind the rise of national and community service and its future prospects is much richer and more complex. Some of the initial building blocks were set into place outside the government over the last decade. The foundation rests on the bedrock of American society and history.

What has happened in recent years is a convergence of three forces in American society that gave shape to the 1990 and 1993 legislation and provided the momentum that made passage of the legislation possible. The first of these forces is a youth service movement initially organized in the early 1980s by a dedicated cadre of individuals and small organizations outside government. The second is the older and much broader tradition of volunteerism in American society, which Alexis de Tocqueville observed and wrote about as a unique feature of American democracy in 1832. The third is the concept of national service, with its own distinctive intellectual history and powerful program antecedents in the Peace Corps and Depression-era Civilian Conservation Corps, which incubated within the Democratic Leadership Council of which Bill Clinton was an early member.

This essay is an effort to sketch a fuller picture of the origins of national service and the 1993 legislation, the social movement that they reflect, and the direction in which they are headed. It also examines

52

unresolved policy issues related to the programmatic directions and future of national and community service, some of which the 1993 legislation seems likely to resolve and some of which it may very well exacerbate.

The Youth Service Movement

In the early 1980s a coordinated effort to engage more young people in national and community service coalesced out of several independent efforts to multiply the number of domestic youth service corps and to spread service learning programs in the nation's schools, colleges, and universities.

The youth corps effort was coordinated by an independent sector organization, the Human Environment Center, then led by Syd Howe and Margaret Rosenberry. Only a handful of domestic youth corps existed at the time. They were state conservation corps that had survived the discontinuation of federal funding for the Young Adult Conservation Corps during the first year of the Reagan Presidency. These conservation corps originally had been created as arms of that federal program. They engaged young people — most of them out of school and unemployed — on a full-time basis for a year or more in state conservation activities. The most prominent was the California Conservation Corps, with the memorable motto of "hard work, low pay, miserable conditions." The California corps was organized in 1976 under Democratic governor Jerry Brown and later made a permanent state agency by Republican governor George Dukmajeian.

The leadership of the Human Environment Center believed that these scattered programs represented a powerful way of socializing young people, especially "marginalized" youth, while delivering needed conservation work in a cost-effective manner. Several state legislatures in addition to California agreed with this policy perspective to the extent of providing modest continuation funding after the federal funds dried up. These included Pennsylvania, Ohio, Wisconsin, Washington, and a few others. The goal of the Human Environment Center was to form a national association of the conservation corps that could work for their survival and seek to replicate the basic model in additional states.

By the mid-1980s the conservation corps model had been adapted to several urban settings in California to engage inner-city youth in conservation and other community service activities. The pioneer urban corps were the San Francisco Conservation Corps and the East Bay Conservation Corps, each a small nongovernmental program with entrepreneurial leadership. During the same period, the New York City

53

Volunteer Corps (CVC) was created with a different mission from the conservation corps. Although funded by the City Council, CVC was chartered as an independent national service corporation for the explicit purpose of demonstrating the feasibility of national service programming at a local level. CVC was sponsored initially by Mayor Ed Koch, a national service advocate since his years as a U.S. Congressman, and was organized to focus on human service activities.

Soon afterward, in Boston, two recent Harvard Law School graduates, Michael Brown and Alan Khazei, took the urban youth corps concept a step further by establishing City Year. The program's motto was "In the spirit of an urban Peace Corps." City Year was entirely privately funded by foundations, corporations, and individuals. It also differed from other domestic youth corps up to that time by achieving a carefully balanced enrollment of young people from diverse economic and racial backgrounds. The founders of City Year had served as staff assistants in the U.S. Congress; one had been on the staff of the New York City Volunteer Corps. Both believed fervently in the wider possibilities of national youth service and defined City Year as a demonstration for a potentially much larger national service program.

Looking to eventual federal legislation, many of the individual conservation and service corps were carefully building political support and publicizing their achievements. The City Volunteer Corps gained editorial support from the *New York Times* as an effective national service demonstration. The San Francisco Conservation Corps found a powerful political ally and advocate in then-Mayor Dianne Feinstein. City Year struck gold in capturing the attention of Senator Edward Kennedy, who would become so crucial for the national legislation ahead. During the 1992 presidential campaign, candidate Bill Clinton visited the City Year program and declared it a model of his national service vision for the nation. During the early months of the transition and Clinton Presidency, the President was frequently televised wearing his City Year sweatshirt on morning jogs.

By the late 1980s some 50 state and local conservation and service corps were thriving across the country. They were linked together by the National Association of Service and Conservation Corps (NASCC), now independent from the Human Environment Center. These corps would be highly influential in shaping and bringing political support to the 1990 and 1993 federal legislation. Because "seeing is believing," they offered tangible program models and a body of knowledge about how to operate effective youth corps outside a framework of direct federal administration (unlike the federally administered Peace Corps, VISTA, and Depression-era Civilian Conservation Corps). Their leadership and founders possessed an independent vision and a sense of momentum that were not fueled by federal funding.

During the same period, substantial momentum was being generated for expanded youth service programming in the nation's schools, colleges, and universities. On a scattered basis, community service activities have existed for many years in some of the country's institutions of higher education. Several influential higher education leaders were strong advocates for the social significance of such programs as the Peace Corps and VISTA and, more broadly, for the power of national and community service to shape positive civic values in each generation of American youth.

Early in the 1980s a group of college and university presidents organized an association, Campus Compact, under the sponsorship of the Education Commission of the States. The goal of Campus Compact was to advocate for the importance of civic values and community service as a fundamental purpose of higher education in America. The ticket for admission to Campus Compact was a personal commitment by a college or university president to upgrade community service programming on his or her own campus. The membership grew quickly to more than 200 institutions, and Campus Compact associations soon were organized in a number of states.

At roughly the same time, college students and recent graduates formed a grassroots association of young people called the Campus Outreach Opportunity League (COOL). Their mission was to advocate for community service projects and more active student leadership among undergraduates throughout the country. While Campus Compact brought hundreds of college and university presidents, deans, and administrators into the effort to push national and community service to the forefront of the American agenda, COOL brought thousands of students into the gathering force. Both organizations and their local members also were making important advances in know-how about local community service programming quality.

Parallel efforts also were under way in precollegiate education. Some of the nation's junior and senior high schools, particularly private Catholic and Quaker schools, have operated student community service programs for decades. Some require minimum service hours or service learning courses as a condition of graduation. In 1983, Ernest Boyer proposed in a widely read education reform book, *High School: A Report on Sec-*

ondary Education in America, that community service be made a fundamental element of the high school curriculum throughout the country. Still, only a small percentage of public school students were participating in community service activities as an aspect of their formal schooling.

In the 1980s several nonprofit organizations began to take up the cause of precollegiate community service programming and to provide technical assistance to schools and teachers. The Constitutional Rights Foundation (CRF) organized community service demonstration programs in a number of Los Angeles urban public schools. CRF also developed, published, and nationally disseminated community service guidebooks. The National Youth Leadership Council (NYLC), based in Minnesota, organized workshops and annual conferences for educators interested in service learning. NYLC had a particularly strong influence on schooling throughout the state of Minnesota and, through its president, Jim Kielsmeier, on the elaboration of service learning doctrines nationally. The Thomas Jefferson Forum organized community service programs in schools throughout the greater Boston area and later statewide in Massachusetts. A Maryland Student Service Alliance assisted with program development in the schools of that state and was instrumental in passage of the first state-level mandatory student service requirement.

As all these youth service program activities began to gain momentum, several national foundations with long-standing interest in youth development or policies related to the transition to adulthood in American society, particularly for "marginalized youth," began playing a pivotal funding role. The Ford Foundation led the way. In 1984 the president of the foundation, Franklin Thomas, made an important speech about national and community service, titled "National Service: An Aspect of Youth Development." He described national service as "a question embedded in a larger question. How should a free and advanced society organize itself to help its children become adults?" Thomas advocated a decentralized, grassroots approach as a policy foundation. He cautioned that "we should not try to erect an elaborate edifice from abstract blueprints and untested assumptions," and instead recommended, "National service should be allowed to grow organically, from many different seeds in many different soils."

Earlier, in 1978-79, Ford had funded a private commission at the Potomac Institute, the Committee for the Study of National Service, which published a widely discussed report, *Youth and the Needs of the Nation*. That commission was led by Harris Wofford, then president of Bryn Mawr College. By 1985, Ford was providing funding to national nonprofit organizations that were seeking to spread youth service programming and to establish a foundation for national policy. Among the nonprofit groups were the Human Environment Center, Campus Compact, and the Constitutional Rights Foundation. Having served as staff director for the Potomac Institute national service project, I was hired by Ford in 1984-85 to survey activities across the country and to advise Ford on a more cohesive grant-making strategy to build a decentralized foundation for national and community service. The Mott and Kellogg foundations, among others, soon joined Ford in providing substantial funding for the activities under way.

In 1986 Ford provided a grant to establish Youth Service America (YSA) with the mission of connecting the leadership of the seminal youth corps, service learning programs, and interested national organizations to explore common goals, best programming practices, and a cohesive policy framework for national advocacy. In 1987 and 1988, YSA convened workshops and conferences to begin to hammer out a common policy framework and advocacy strategy for a national youth service rooted in the emerging national network of innovative programs. The most important step was organizing a Working Group on Youth Service Policy for outreach to the 1988 presidential campaigns and other national policymaking circles. The Working Group included Campus Compact, NASCC, COOL, the National Youth Leadership Council, the William T. Grant Foundation, and a growing circle of other organizations. A set of position papers on national youth service was prepared for the incoming Bush Administration and Democratic advocates for national service in the United States Senate.

Youth Service America also served as the initial fiscal agent for City Year and organized the national replication of the Youth Volunteer Corps, a service program for younger teenagers piloted and now headquartered in Kansas City. YSA also organized an annual national promotion campaign for youth service, called National Youth Service Day, assisted by COOL, the Jefferson Awards, and the U.S. Conference of Mayors.

Collectively, the activities of what came to be called "the youth service movement" formed a tangible programming foundation, a policy framework, and a constituency base for the federal government activity that was soon to follow.

Federal Initiatives in 1988, 1989, and 1990

By 1988 elements of both national political parties were seriously interested in national service, but they came to the concept with widely differing policy perspectives. The Republican Party has a long-standing interest, broadly, in the ethic of volunteerism in American society. Former Republican Governor George Romney of Michigan was instrumental in establishing a network of volunteer centers across the country, and it is not uncommon for Republican governors to establish an office of volunteerism in state government. The policy section of the 1988 presidential campaign of George Bush began to take an active interest in the idea of national youth service. They maintained contact with the Working Group on Youth Service Policy and welcomed suggestions and concept papers, though they would not schedule the candidate for visits to youth corps sites, an early signal of reservations about stipended, full-time service corps.

Near the end of the 1988 campaign, on October 5, George Bush made a speech in Compton, California, promising to establish a YES (Youth Entering Service) to America Foundation if elected President. He further announced that he would "request from Congress up to $100 million in federal funds for the foundation to match on a one-to-one basis private donations up to $100 million." The speech and subsequent press notices stirred great excitement in the youth service movement, particularly the plan "to establish a challenge grant program designed to spur more young people to serve their communities as a continuing and routine part of their daily lives in high school, college, and after graduation." The Vice President proposed that:

> The $200 million generated in this effort will give new meaning to the term "public-private partnership" and will be dedicated to creating local community and school-based programs to involve teenagers and young adults in volunteer service to meet the needs of their communities. . . . YES to America will be a program of opportunities for national service to meet our country's most pressing needs and to encourage young Americans to engage in the building of a better society.

After winning the election, the Bush Administration quickly created a White House Office of National Service. What took shape in that office was not the youth program outlined in the California speech, but a broader "Points of Light Initiative" designed to publicize and strengthen the rich fabric of volunteer activities across the country. On June 22, in New York City, the President announced his intention to create a Points of Light Foundation, for which he would seek $25 million annually from the Congress. The thrust of President Bush's national service initiative was to encourage the ethic of volunteerism in the private sector and among individual volunteers, utilizing the bully pulpit of the presidency. The Administration distanced itself from the youth corps program network and a federally administered grants program. However, President Bush was drawn somewhat deeper into national service and the national youth service movement through the congressional actions that led to the National and Community Service Act of 1990.

As the Points of Light Initiative was taking shape, and even before the 1988 presidential campaign, a number of Senators and House Members were drawing up national youth service legislation. Senators Barbara Mikulski, Claiborne Pell, Dale Bumpers, Daniel Moynihan, and Sam Nunn each introduced a version of national service legislation in the Senate. In the House, Dave McCurdy, Connie Morella, Robert Torricelli, Gerry Sikorski, and Leon Panetta introduced bills.

Within the political parties, the most systematic policy work on national service was being done by the Democratic Leadership Council, a splinter group of the Democratic Party seeking to shape a fresh policy agenda that could bring the party back to presidential power. The DLC laid out its national service plan in a 1988 publication, *Citizenship and National Service*, drawing in part from the youth corps and service learning models already under way in the independent sector. However, the DLC envisioned large-scale federal funding for national youth service and, on the model of the GI Bill, linkage between national service and federal financial support for higher education students. When the DLC plan was introduced in the Senate in 1989 by Senator Sam Nunn (S. 3, The Citizenship and National Service Act of 1988), it received enormous national publicity. It also met with a firestorm of opposition. Higher education and civil rights groups opposed the bill because of the linkage between federal loans and national service, which they viewed as unfair coercion of low-income students. Conservative groups attacked the bill as a disguised federal welfare or employment program along the lines of the discredited Comprehensive Employment Training Act.

None of the national service bills introduced in 1988 and 1989 had serious prospects for passage. They reflected the old paradigm of government-dominated national service. However, with a White House Office of National Service and a nongovernmental grassroots youth service movement under way, sufficient momentum had been achieved to make some more innovative and constituency-based form of national service legislation a distinct possibility.

Senator Edward Kennedy, as chairman of the Senate Labor and Human Resources Committee, undertook the task of reviewing all the national service bills in the Senate along with the Bush Administration's Points of Light proposal to see if a new piece of legislation could be crafted that could meet the interests of the various players and gain majority support in the Congress. Over several months of consultations with the youth service movement, official hearings, and private political negotiations, Kennedy's effort produced the National and Community Service Act of 1990, which the Working Group on Youth Service Policy dubbed "the omnibus bill" and played a key role in shaping. With support from President Bush, the Senate bill passed with a strong, bipartisan majority, 75 to 21. The measure was authorized $287 million over three years. After some initial difficulties, parallel legislation was drafted in the House Committee on Education and Labor and passed the House by voice vote.

The 1990 legislation essentially created a modest federal grants program to the states in support of multiple programming streams for national and community service. Subtitles of the act directed funding to service learning programs at both precollegiate and higher education levels, to full-time conservation and service corps, and to a select number of national service demonstration programs at the state level. The bill also provided direct funding for President Bush's proposed Points of Light Foundation. A small Commission on National and Community Service, nominated by the President, was established to administer the legislation. The governors of states were required to designate a state agency to develop and submit comprehensive state proposals and administer any funds received. Funding decisions were made by the federal commission on a competitive basis.

However, President Bush did not nominate a commission during the first year, resulting in a loss of that year's funds. There was still substantial resistance within the Bush Administration to the subtitles of the legislation that provided funding for full-time corps and national service demonstrations, called by opponents the "oxymoron of paid volunteerism." But these subtitles enjoyed support not only from Democratic Senators, but also from a number of Republican Senators. Finally, in the second year of authorization, the President nominated a commission and the legislation became operational.

The 1990 act brought dramatic structural changes to the youth service movement. The legislation gave state agencies — in most cases extensions of state government — the role of dispensing the field's new financial resource of federal funds. The only exceptions were higher education programming funds and a small pool of discretionary funds, from which the commission could make direct grants. The grant-making by state agencies seems to have for the most part reinforced and enriched the youth service movement's precollegiate and youth corps programming streams.

The national service demonstration subtitle brought the most dramatic changes to the building blocks for national youth service. The federal commission, limited by the legislation to state agency applications, selected only one existing youth corps as a national service demonstration model, the City Year program in Boston. The grant provided significant federal funding for local expansion of City Year and for preparations to undertake multiple-site, national replication. The other national service demonstrations funded by the federal commission were entirely new programs operated by state governments: the Georgia Peach Corps, the Delta Service Corps (Arkansas, Mississippi, and Alabama in combination), Volunteer Maryland, and Pennsylvania Service Corps. The programmatic definition of national and community service was enlarged by these demonstration programs to be inclusive of volunteers across a spectrum of ages. It also included individual placements in the style of VISTA or the Peace Corps to generate a "multiplier effect" of local volunteerism. Other than the City Year program, the federal commission gave state governments center stage for national service demonstrations and bypassed the youth service movement's other entrepreneurial program models. This situation was to some extent corrected during the second and last round of commission funding.

The policy directions brought about by the 1990 federal legislation had multiple consequences. National and community service programming was moved more deeply into the councils of federal and state government. The basic programming streams of the youth service movement, precollegiate and higher education service learning models and youth corps models, were reinforced. The national service demonstrations in particular were more inclusive of volunteers of diverse ages. The legislation also provided $5 million annually in funding for the new Points of Light Foundation, which absorbed the network of volunteer centers across the country and began working on their development and expansion. There also were less formal but powerful efforts by the federal commission and others in the field to ensure racial and ethnic diversity of participation in national and community service, at both volunteer and leadership levels, and to promote and cultivate a "youth voice" and young leaders in the field. Some of the most interesting emerging community service models were being led by young entrepreneurs in their 20s, reaching out to involve their peers: City Year, Teach for America,

Public Allies, the Youth Volunteer Corps of America, the Urban Service Project, and others.

Separate from the federal legislation, but probably accelerated by its visibility, multiple sources of additional funds began flowing at all levels – foundations, corporations, state and local governments, and individual donors. In sum, these other investments were probably more than triple the size of the federal investment.

As the country entered the 1992 presidential election year, the momentum behind national and community service was still accelerating. A leadership summit supported by the MacArthur Foundation and organized by Youth Service America concluded that the central challenge to the field had become managing its growth. The variety of local, state, and national models was richer than ever before, with the dual impact of the grants program of the federal commission and entrepreneurial leaders across the country creating new initiatives. The definitions of the core principles and parameters of national and community service were in a state of flux.

The Clinton Initiative and 1993 Legislation

The Clinton campaign's march to victory in the 1992 presidential election brought with it the conceptual framework for national service that incubated within the Democratic Leadership Council and to which Bill Clinton is passionately committed. City Year probably represents the clearest expression of the new President's vision: diverse and idealistic young Americans between the ages of 17 and 25 organized into a disciplined service corps for a year or more of full-time community service. Essentially a domestic Peace Corps, their service is devoted to dual goals of citizenship development and solving basic social and environmental problems in exchange for financial support for their higher education.

However, Clinton's vision also is enormously ambitious. The President clearly imagines hundreds of thousands of young people engaged in service each year, a program on the scale of President Roosevelt's Civilian Conservation Corps or the contemporary military services, with a complementary trust fund making higher education more accessible to the young people who participate. The program of President Clinton's original vision would cost billions of federal dollars or some combination of federal and private dollars. It is a vision that contrasts markedly with the Bush Administration's vision of nurturing more traditional, private-sector volunteerism. It also differs in at least two respects from the policy framework advanced by the youth service movement: 1) the centrality of government influence and 2) linkage to federal financing of student aid for higher education.

As the Clinton staff took over the White House Office of National Service in early 1993, the 1990 act was nearing the end of its three-year authorization; and the congressional legislative mechanisms were being geared up for reauthorization. The task before the key committees was to adapt the framework of the 1990 legislation to the new President's ambitious proposals and to incorporate recommendations for policy improvements coming from the field experience of the last couple years. This task had to be achieved while holding a bipartisan majority in the Senate. The situation in the Senate was highly contentious, as the Republican minority was testing the will and skill of the Clinton Administration on every legislative front, including national and community service. Meanwhile, the nongovernmental organizations for national and community service had organized themselves into a formidable reauthorization coalition, housed at Youth Service America. The Coalition for National and Community Service, with more than 120 member organizations, focused its efforts on helping to frame and pass the new legislation.

The core legislative interests of the Clinton Office of National Service initially were focused on fulfilling the President's campaign pledge of a national service trust fund. Early discussions revolved around seeking a four- or five-year authorization of between $7.5 and $9 billion, inclusive of program costs, for a large number of full-time national service positions plus a higher education trust fund to award scholarships or loan forgiveness of up to $10,000 for each year of service. In addition to the question of whether this was politically feasible in the Congress, there were other questions. What would happen with the service learning subtitles of the 1990 act? Would the federal commission continue to administer the new legislation or would some new kind of entity be created? How would the Peace Corps and ACTION fit into the new national service scheme? What would happen to the cross-generation national service demonstrations of the earlier legislation? What roles would the states, cities, and independent organizations have in the framework of the new legislation?

Before the legislative process began to resolve these and other issues, Clinton's Office of National Service decided that they should not wait until 1994 before the President's national service initiative became visible to the public. There was much talk about how quickly President Kennedy's Peace Corps volunteers had reached their field assignments after Kennedy took office in 1961. In short order, a preview of Clinton's plan was designed for the summer of 1993. The operations of the federal commission created by the 1990 legislation made this "Summer of Service" possible. Within a remarkably short time the commission solicited funding proposals for 1,500 summer community service positions and funded some 30 local programs for immediate implementation, with an initial week of collective national training on Treasure Island in San Francisco before returning to local sites. This venture generated intense activity and generally favorable publicity, but it was a side show to the major legislative arena. However, because of a host of logistical problems and ideological disputes, the Summer of Service did sober the Office of National Service by showing just how difficult it was going be to design a system of national and community service that could capture President Clinton's ideals, be effectively implemented, and become widely viewed as successful.

Senate and House committees, working with the Office of National Service and consulting with interested Republican members of Congress and with the Coalition for National and Community Service, pieced together the National and Community Service Trust Act of 1993. Experience with the 1990 legislation made this process far more efficient than would otherwise have been possible. However, Republicans in the Senate, led by Senator Nancy Kassebaum, also quickly pieced together an alternative piece of legislation to lock horns over the differing policy perspectives of the political parties.

Senator Kennedy's and Congressman Ford's coordinated legislation, S. 919 and H.R. 2010, established the basic framework that eventually passed the Congress and was signed into law by the President in September 1993. Compromises to build majority support drastically lowered the authorization figures. In the end, the new act provides for an expanding three-year authorization of $300 million, $500 million, and $700 million, a total of $1.5 billion. The program will be administered by a new federal Corporation for National and Community Service with an executive appointed by the President and a board of directors nominated by the President. ACTION and a separately authorized Civilian Community Corps will be folded into the corporation, but the Peace Corps will remain independent. Each state will establish a Commission on National and Community Service governed by a board of directors appointed by the governor to submit comprehensive state grant proposals to the federal corporation and to administer the funds received. The federal corporation also will administer the trust fund of $4,725 higher education awards to individuals who complete a term of service. Of the remaining funds, one-third will go to states on a population formula basis and one-third will be reserved for grants to states on a competitive basis. The other one-third will be awarded directly by the corporation on a competitive basis to subentities of states, nonprofit organizations, or federal agencies.

The centerpiece of the legislation is the AmeriCorps program, the core Clinton plan for full-time service positions, expanding from approximately 20,000 to 70,000 over three years; but pools of funds also will be available for part-time service learning programs and other community service activities outside the AmeriCorps scheme. Annual funding of $5 million was set aside for the Points of Light Foundation to promote volunteerism.

The new legislation is different from the 1990 legislation in some important respects but generally continues the earlier legislative framework. The National and Community Service Trust Act of 1993 passed the House easily. There was a pitched battle in the Senate, revolving primarily around the overall level of federal funding, the size of the post-service award, and the dominant role of the federal government in administering the legislation. In the end, the Senate vote was 58 to 41, a much narrower margin than the 75 to 21 vote for the 1990 legislation. Bipartisan support for federal assistance in building a system of national and community service had grown thinner. But the level of federal funding and overall momentum across the country for national and community service has grown considerably stronger.

The Road Ahead

Since the early investments by the Ford and other foundations and the advocacy and policy groundwork by the Working Group on Youth Service Policy, the progress of national and community service programming and policy has been impressive. Solid models that engage large numbers of young people and others in community service are thriving; many have arisen from entrepreneurial rather than bureaucratic origins. The field's leadership circle of program operators, team leaders, trainers, and young advocates has been vastly enlarged. The conservation and service corps have begun to document and evaluate their youth development and community service achievements. Surveys show that attitudes among college students about community service and civic values have become much more positive since the early 1980s. Two successive Administrations, the Congress, and many states have been deeply engaged. The scope of publicity about youth service and volunteerism has grown substantially. The work of the federal commission established by the 1990 legislation is widely viewed as highly successful, and the new federal corporation has just begun its work.

But there are many challenges and problems ahead, not all of them related to fine-tuning implementation of the 1993 act, as important as that is. It is difficult to see the way to fulfilling President Clinton's powerful campaign pledge to make higher education more available to any young person who is willing to contribute a year or two of full-time service, with a special political emphasis on middle-class families. Under the new legislation, the AmeriCorps program will enroll 20,000 participants in its first year, expanding to as many as 70,000 by its third year. But a national service system enrolling hundreds of thousands of participants would cost many billions of dollars. The early funding strategy proposed by the Democratic Leadership Council — folding existing federal student loan funds into a national service trust fund — faces strong opposition from interest groups, even from some of the primary supporters of national service. The federal budget deficit mitigates against large new appropriations for the trust fund for many years.

Two other general funding strategies hold some prospects for expanding the national service trust fund. One is progressively capturing and converting other existing federal agency authorizations to national service programming. Examples include college work-study funds in the Department of Education, Department of Labor employment and training funds, and federal low-income housing development funds in the Department of Housing and Urban Development. This will require some fancy footwork by the Clinton Administration and allies in Congress, but Senators Harris Wofford and David Boren, among others, are already at work on the strategy.

A second strategy would be to begin to match federal investments in a national service trust fund with private sources. For example, colleges and universities could be encouraged to build trust funds for their own students who participate in national service, aggregating across the country a pool of private funding that begins to match the federal contribution. If sold on the value of national service to young people and to the country, national foundations, community foundations, and wealthy individuals might also make substantial contributions to a web of trust funds. State and local governments and other kinds of institutions also might get into the game.

The ultimate challenge of bringing the national service trust vision to full realization is not so much available capital as building a public mandate. Americans spend billions on alcohol and tobacco, among many other products. If the national service trust can prove itself to the American people to be a valuable investment, like highways or Social Security, they might well support its funding on the scale envisioned by President Clinton.

Another key challenge is overcoming seemingly intractable ideological differences. Despite the substantial bipartisan compromises worked out during Senate debate of the 1993 act, Senators Nancy Kassebaum and John Danforth voted against the legislation with a majority of Senate Republicans. Their opposition was rooted in deep skepticism about an expanded federal role in voluntary community service activities and strong reservations about federally stipended service corps in particular. Doug Bandow of the Cato Institute, in the *Wall Street Journal*, attacked national service as a "boondoggle" that will "expand federal power, politicize the independent sector, increase an already nightmarish deficit, and siphon tens of thousands of young people out of productive private labor and into make-work projects."

Like Kassebaum and Danforth, Bandow favors "a renewed commitment" to individual service through the family, churches, and civic groups. This is an agenda in many ways consistent with the Points of Light Foundation established by President Bush. Many supporters of traditional volunteerism oppose an activist federal government role through the Corporation for National and Community Service and building a growing national service trust fund for AmeriCorps. Can these differences be bridged?

The intent of the 1990 and 1993 legislation is to decentralize utilization of the federal funds, primarily through the states, in support of a wide range of state and local community service activities, some part time and some full time. Will this federalism strategy preclude Bandow's predictions of "make-work projects" and "politicization of volunteerism"? A great deal will depend on the program quality and scope of public support for the community service activities that evolve over the next several years, particularly for the AmeriCorps programs that are likely to get the greatest publicity and the sharpest scrutiny.

Philosophical and partisan opponents of an activist federal government are unlikely to be converted by any measure of success with the federal corporation's grants program. But among opinion makers and the broader public, national and community service programs will swiftly develop a reputation at local and national levels for the value of their contributions to the young people who participate and to the substantive domains in which the service is rendered. If the "make-work" charge begins to stick, as it did with many social programs of the Great Society period, the AmeriCorps program is doomed. If the federal corporation reflects a narrowly driven partisan agenda, instead of working in close collaboration with the nongovernmental sector on its program and policy choices, then Kassebaum, Danforth, and Bandow will turn out to have been right. But the outcomes they fear are not preordained.

In Washington's inner circles of debate about the prospects of the AmeriCorps program, a consensus is emerging about the key variables of practical success over the next couple years. The program must be a success in its youth development objectives, variously expressed in citizenship or employment terms. It must be successful in achieving measurable results with community service objectives, probably in the context of a few clear national priorities, a task complicated by a decentralized approach to programming. It must be successful in educational terms, which means assisting growing numbers of young people with higher education financing. It must win the public relations battle of a favorable perception by the taxpayers.

At the hands-on program level, another huge challenge to the success of national and community service is the management of race and class interests and conflicts. One glittering promise of national service is, through deliberate integration and teamwork, to help make diversity an asset for American society, rather than a divisive factor. Does this mean that all national service programs should be multicultural and multiracial? Or does it mean that the overall system of national service becomes a mosaic that "looks like America," where some particular programs might be racially or socioeconomically homogeneous to reflect the demographics of their particular communities?

The Administration's 1993 Summer of Service program ran head on into the American race conundrum. These issues were described in a recent *Newsweek* article by Steven Waldman, an astute reporter preparing a book on the Clinton national service initiative. Waldman contrasted President Clinton's ideal of a national service program of smooth, integrated teamwork with the Summer of Service reality of intense racial affiliation and group conflict. Summer of Service participants were at least 75% minorities, predominantly African-American, in a society that is currently about 25% minorities. Several of the Summer of Service local programs with "indigenous community leadership" declared less

68

interest in "community service" than in community empowerment and economic development. Like university campuses that have adopted the multicultural ideal, multiculturalism brought a very uneasy mix of racial affiliations, perspectives, and agendas to the Summer of Service.

Suzanne Goldsmith's new book, *City Year* (1993), documents the experience of one racially diverse team in that much-publicized youth corps and shows just how demanding it can be to mix divergent ethnic and class backgrounds to carry out effective community service projects.

At a national policy level, it seems unlikely that American taxpayers will become attached to a national service program that does not serve the interests of the majority, as well as the minorities, in American society. Some consensus policy guidelines about race and class will have to be worked out — and carried out — and an "image" for national service must be established that gains sustained support from the American public.

Another related issue that will have to be addressed is the extent to which national service programs will balance employment and job-training aims with citizenship service aims. Which groups will be targeted for participation in the program? Which organizations will operate the programs? Whose interests will be served? There is already substantial dissension within the existing youth corps network over these issues and aims.

As the national and community service field advances with the new infusion of federal funds and leadership, it will not be easy to hold together the mix of perspectives represented by traditional volunteerism, full-time and stipended youth corps, and service learning programs. The movement has promoted the slogan that "all streams of service must advance together," but that is easier said than done. The 1993 legislation, like the 1990 act, encompasses the potential for advancing a multidimensional paradigm for national and community service; but the federal corporation and state commissions will have to make all the right moves. The balance of forces in American society also will encourage attention to each of the major perspectives.

What is the proper balance between governmental and nongovernmental leadership and administration of national and community service? Ford Foundation President Franklin Thomas has proposed that national service "should be allowed to grow organically, from many different seeds in many different soils." The Working Group on Youth Service Policy, composed of private-sector organizations active in the youth service movement, has sought a partnership with government, but not dominance by government. In contrast, Roosevelt's Civilian Conservation Corps and Kennedy's Peace Corps have been not only federally funded but also federally administered programs. The "new national service" is evolving around a different paradigm: a broad diversity of programs reaching varied age groups with different intensities of participation, with mixes of government and private funding, and using creative combinations of government and private-sector collaboration and administration.

Some seasoned veterans feel that the momentum behind national and community service, which draws from some of the deepest traditions of our culture, is now irreversible. I disagree. The greatest challenge to national service, to the extent that it is driven by federal funding, is the possibility that it could suddenly collapse with a change in administration or the political tide. We know from experience with federal social programs over the last 30 years that most government-driven social programs are unlikely to last for very long as presidential administrations and political tides change course. Yet the core goals of national service – as articulated by William James, William F. Buckley, Franklin Thomas, Bill Clinton, and many others – are long-term: to create an enduring rite of passage for young Americans into active citizenship and to diffuse the ethic of citizen service more broadly and fully into each generation. It is a task of building a new institution in which not only government but other major institutions of American society are stakeholders. The 1993 legislation contains the possibility of advancing this purpose, but the leadership of the federal corporation and the state commissions will have to focus very squarely on this longer-term outcome. Equally important, the service movement, already much broader than the legislation, will have to ensure that the long-term goal is kept at the forefront of both governmental and nongovernmental efforts.

In my view, the key to the future of national service, in addition to the quality of programs that evolve across the country, is that national and community service evolve not as another big-government program, but as an essentially nongovernmental program in which the government is one of many investors.

National Service: Utopias Revisited

By Doug Bandow

Doug Bandow is a Senior Fellow at the Cato Institute and a former Special Assistant to President Ronald Reagan.

He also is a nationally syndicated columnist and the author of The Politics of Plunder: Misgovernment in Washington.

In his State of the Union speech, President Bill Clinton proposed more than just higher taxes and additional spending as part of his curious approach toward deficit reduction. He also promised to make his vision of national service a reality. In the President's mind, not only is Washington to take a larger share of people's earnings to use in more "appropriate" ways. The state also is apparently to guide the young into more "appropriate" pursuits as well.

National service has long been a favorite utopian scheme. Eight decades ago William James wrote of the need for a "moral equivalent of war," in which all young men would be required to work for the community. He argued that "the martial virtues, although originally gained by the race through war, are absolute and permanent human goods," and that national service provided a method of instilling those same values in peacetime. "Our gilded youths would be drafted off," he wrote, "to get the childishness knocked out of them, and to come back into society with healthier sympathies and soberer ideas." Anachronistic though his vision may seem today, his rhetoric has become the touchstone for national service advocates. In succeeding decades a host of philosophers, policy analysts, and politicians proffered their own proposals for either voluntary or mandatory national service. And some of these initiatives have been turned into law: military conscription, the Civilian Conservation Corps, the Peace Corps, and ACTION, for instance.

In 1988 the Democratic Leadership Council, to which Governor Bill Clinton belonged, advocated a Citizens Corps of 800,000 or more young people to clean up parks and handle police paperwork. The system would be run by a Corporation for National Service, which would set the level of benefits for participants and offer an education/housing voucher. Underlying the proposal was an assumption of mass moral decadence that had to be rectified by the federal government. We live in a "prevailing climate of moral indolence," contended the DLC, where "such venerable civic virtues as duty and self-sacrifice and compassion toward one's less fortunate neighbors are seldom invoked."

Candidate Clinton was too interested in being elected to criticize the voters in those terms, so he used more positive rhetoric to propose allowing perhaps 250,000 or so people annually to work off their student loans through approved government service (once in office he reduced the total to 150,000). His initiative, he explained, would allow everyone who wanted to go to school to do so, while having them give something back to the community. Superficially, at least, it sounded like a win-win proposition. In practice, however, his program, a more limited version of which was approved by Congress, will likely pour billions of dollars into make-work jobs while reinforcing the entitlement mentality that pervades our society.

What Is National Service?

National service has always generated strong approval in opinion polls, largely because it means different things to different people. The concept of "service" to the nation seems difficult to fault, and everyone imagines that the "service" that results will be of the form and provided in the manner that they prefer. Thus, a century ago Edward Bellamy used his novel *Looking Backward* to propose drafting an industrial army of both men and women for life; in 1910 William James urged conscription of young men into the most unpleasant of work, such as construction, fishing, and steel-making. The so-called preparedness movement pressed for mandatory military training and service before the onset of World War I. Radical Randolph Bourne later proposed forcing young men and women to provide two years of service before the age of 20. Universal military training received wide endorsement after World War II, and Congress reimposed military conscription after only a one-year interregnum. Defense Secretary Robert McNamara advocated tying civilian service to the draft in the early 1960s. Sociologist Margaret Mead advocated a universal program that "would replace for girls, even more than for boys, marriage as the route away from the parental home."

Since then the proposals have come fast and furious. Don Eberly of the National Service Secretariat has spent years pressing for a service program, while carefully sidestepping the question of whether it should be mandatory. Charles Moskos of Northwestern University pushed a civilian adjunct to the draft before the creation of the All-Volunteer Force in 1973 and most recently has presented a detailed voluntary program. Moskos nevertheless retains a preference for civilian conscription, admitting that "if I could have a magic wand I would be for a compulsory system." (Also mandatory, though in a different way, is the service requirement for high school graduation now imposed by the state of Maryland and roughly 200 local school jurisdictions.) Dozens of bills were proposed in the 1980s to create commissions, hand out grants, reestablish the Civilian Conservation Corps and Works Progress Administration, initiate other new service agencies, and pay part-time volunteers. Most serious was the Democratic Leadership Council's initiative, which Congress turned into an omnibus grant program, along with the Commission on National and Community Service. The issue had largely died until the Los Angeles riots caused observers — from the late tennis great Arthur Ashe to *Newsweek* columnist and former colonel David Hackworth to Bush campaign aide James Pinkerton — to press for different forms of national service. More important, candidate Clinton began inserting the idea into his stump speeches.

Clinton's Scheme

According to President Clinton, "you could bet your bottom dollar" that his program would "make it possible for every person in this country who wants to, to go to college." He proposed, as one of his top five priorities, creating the National Service Trust Fund. Everyone, irrespective of their parents' income, could borrow for their education; they would repay their loans either through federal withholding from future wages or by "serving their communities for one or two years doing work their country needs." After the election some advisers, like Moskos, pressed the President to consider also an alternative approach, allowing high school graduates to earn college tuition vouchers through community service.

However, deficit concerns caused the Administration to back away quickly from President Clinton's most ambitious campaign musings, even though, explained then-White House spokesman George Stephanopoulos, the President "intends to fulfill his commitment to build a national service plan." In a speech at Rutgers University, Clinton proposed to start with a pilot program, to be expanded to as many as 150,000 participants or more, who would receive two years of tuition for every year of work. Apparently students could work either before or after attending college. Total benefits — and whether participants' salaries would all be equal or would reflect the total amount of aid received and forgiven, which would obviously be much greater for someone attending an Ivy League school than for someone attending a state university — were originally unspecified. In return, explained President Clinton:

> We'll ask you to help our police forces across the nation, training members a new police corps, that will walk beats and work with neighborhoods and build the kind of community ties that will prevent crime from happening in the first place; we'll ask young people to help control pollution and recycle waste, to paint darkened buildings and clean up neighborhoods, to work with senior citizens and combat homelessness and help children in trouble.

Ultimately, the President offered a more limited initiative and Congress approved a further scaled-down version of the Clinton proposal. The newly created AmeriCorps will employ some 20,000 in its first year and up to 100,000 over three years. Full-time participants will receive minimum-wage compensation plus fringe benefits and a tax-free education voucher of $4,725; a part-timer's voucher will be half as large. The Corporation for National and Community Service, subsuming the Commission on National and Community Service and ACTION, will administer AmeriCorps. The corporation is to offer information, technical assistance, and, most important, money to state service programs. The corporation also will promote service learning programs for school children and initiatives involving the elderly. States must create their own commissions on national service and select the programs to be funded by the corporation.

Congress authorized $1.5 billion over three years for the corporation and, in typical fashion, set aside grant money for favored interests and bureaucracies: labor, Indian tribes, the disabled, the elderly, state governments, universities, and state education agencies. The corporation set up shop on 1 October 1993 and now is soliciting proposals for well over $100 million worth of grants for 1994.

There is nothing compulsory about the Clinton proposal, but coercion could follow later. Of course, the President's avoidance of military service during the Vietnam War makes it difficult for him to ever propose such a step. However, such long-time enthusiasts of a manda-

74

tory, universal system as Senator John McCain (R-Ariz.) see voluntary programs as a helpful first step and may continue pressing for their approach with a limited form of national service now the law of the land, especially if "too few" children of privilege and wealth join. After all, Senator Edward Kennedy exulted that "in a sense, the passage of this legislation marks the end of the 'me' era in our national life." But what if the employment of a few thousand people in "public service" projects has no such effect, leaving unreformed the "moral indolence" denounced by the DLC a few years ago? Then he, along with the more conservative Democrats who make up the DLC, also might be moved to support compulsion.

Service is obviously a good thing, which is why so many people feel warm and fuzzy when politicians propose "national service." The issue, however, is service to whom? All of these government programs ultimately assume that citizens are responsible not to each other, but to the state. The proposals suggest that as a price for being born in the United States, one "owes" a year or two of one's life to Washington. Mandatory, universal schemes unabashedly put private lives at the disposal of the government; but most voluntary programs, too, imply a unity of society and state, with work for the latter being equated with service to the former.

Yet Americans have worked in their communities since the nation's founding, and opportunities abound for similar service today. Some 80 million people, roughly one-third of the population, now participate in some volunteer activities. Businesses, churches, and schools have taken the lead in helping to organize their members' efforts. In a cover story, *Newsweek* reported that "many of the old stereotypes are gone. Forget the garden club; today working women are more likely than housewives to give time to good works, and many organizations are creating night and weekend programs for the busy schedules of dual-paycheck couples. Men, too, are volunteering almost as often as women."

Much more could be done, of course. But it would be better for government officials to lead by example, rather than to concoct multi-billion-dollar schemes to encourage what already is occurring. True compassion is going to be taught from the grassroots up, not from Washington down. The underlying assumption of the Clinton program — that there is a debilitating dearth of service that can be remedied only through yet another raid on the taxpayers — is simply false. Moreover, the Clinton program, while cloaked in public-spirited rhetoric, nevertheless relies heavily on economic incentives. Indeed, much of the President's pitch during the campaign was framed in terms of naked self-interest: earning credit toward college tuition.

A second bias held by national service advocates is that "public" service is inherently better than private service. Yet what makes shelving books in a library more laudable or valuable than stocking shelves in a bookstore? A host of private-sector jobs provide enormous public benefits — consider health care professionals, medical and scientific researchers, business entrepreneurs and inventors, and artists. Working in a government-approved "service" job neither entitles one to be morally smug nor means one is producing more of value than the average employee in the private workplace.

Entitlement Mentality

Still, national service proponents rightly point to the problem of an entitlement mentality, the idea that, for instance, students have a right to a taxpayer-paid education. Why should middle-class young people be able to force poor taxpayers to put them through school? The solution, however, is not to say that students are entitled to do so as long as they work for the government for a year or two, but to eliminate the undeserved subsidy. People simply do not have a "right" to a university education, and especially a professional degree, at taxpayer expense.

National service advocates respond with shock. Education, they argue, will be increasingly important in an increasingly technological age. True enough: The greatest divergence in incomes in the 1980s reflected the gulf between those with and without college degrees. However, that increased earning potential primarily benefits the student himself; and the likely lifetime gain of $640,000 should allow him or her to borrow privately. The interest rate may be higher than with today's federal guarantees, but that hardly seems unfair given the added earnings of the student.

Nevertheless, Senator Chris Dodd (D-Conn.), an early supporter of the Clinton program, contends that even middle-class families can ill afford to send their kids to college. That's now accepted as a truism, but it is not obviously correct. More than three-quarters of the best students currently go on to higher education. Qualified students unable to get a college education because of finances are few. Policymakers need to acknowledge that not everyone needs a university degree, and one from a leading school, to find fulfillment in life. Some young people are not academically oriented or interested; others have found more satisfying ways to spend their lives. The federal government shouldn't be pushing them to go to college.

Anyway, the fact that higher education, especially at elite private universities, strains many family budgets is hardly surprising, since the dramatic increase in federal education aid has helped fuel a rapid rise in tuition. Further flooding the education system with money is likely to benefit administrators as much as students. The point is, if there's more money available for schools to collect, they will do so.

Moreover, it is because of free-spending legislators like Dodd that government now takes roughly half of the national income, making it difficult for families to afford higher education. Therefore, politicians worried about middle-class taxpayers should cut special-interest spending, not hike costs by billions of dollars through a national service program. In short, while the jump in federal education assistance in the 1970s undoubtedly helped more students attend college, there is no reason to assume both that these marginal attendees benefited more than the cost of their education and that they could not have afforded school had tuitions not be artificially inflated by the influx of aid and their families' incomes been so sharply reduced by taxes.

The problem with national service is not just theoretical, however. Like every other proposed national service plan, the Clinton proposal is likely to break down in practice. Shortly after his election, the President admitted: "I feel very passionate about [national service,] but there are a lot of factual questions that have to be asked. How much money should everybody be able to borrow a year? What contributions should people's families be expected to make, if any? If you put this into effect, how are you going to keep the colleges and the universities of this country from using it as an excuse to explode tuition even more?" Good questions all, and all go to the viability of any program. Alas, passage of his legislation has not really answered them.

The implementation problems are likely to be enormous. First, President Clinton says that he will not allow any job displacement, which guarantees that participants will not perform the most valuable work to be done. The Democratic Leadership Council's proposed program had the same feature — to forestall opposition from organized labor, the group promised that its program would neither impair existing contracts nor limit the promotion possibilities for existing workers. However, the latter is virtually impossible to enforce: if AmeriCorps members end up at local school districts as teachers and teachers' aides, will the district hire as many other teachers and teachers' aides in the future? Almost any job that might be performed by a municipal union member is likely to be excluded from any national service program or, if not, is likely to generate significant political opposition.

Even assuming this problem can be overcome, national service is not likely to produce significant social benefits. What work would participants do? Past government "service" programs have always been very limited in scope. Advocates of national service like to point to the Peace Corps and VISTA, but these two programs, along with more than 60 state and local programs, involve some 18,000 people. Even during the military draft, the government had little use for the labor of conscientious objectors, placing only 30,000 into service jobs from 1951 to 1965. What will tens of thousands a year more do?

Meet current "unmet social needs," national service advocates respond. Past proponents of national service have tossed around figures ranging up to 5.3 million as to the number of jobs that need to be done. According to one study, for instance, libraries require 200,000 people; education needs six times as many. But as long as human wants are unlimited, the real number of unfilled social "needs," as well as unmet business "needs," is infinite. Labor, however, is not a free resource. Thus, it simply isn't worthwhile to satisfy most of these "unmet" needs. One of the great benefits of the market process is that it balances benefits and costs throughout society, using wages as a signal to determine when activities warrant undertaking. National service would treat some jobs as sacrosanct, while ignoring disfavored alternative tasks that could be performed instead.

Opportunity Costs

Indeed, this may be the crux of the national service debate: the role of opportunity costs. Paying young people their national service's generous compensation — they will receive tuition relief plus salary and health care benefits — to paint "darkened buildings," suggested by the President, or do police paperwork, proposed as part of the DLC's program, or perform other "service" entails forgoing whatever else could be done with that money. Moreover, it involves forgoing whatever else young people could do. "Public service" has a nice ring to it, but there is no reason to believe *a priori* that a dollar going to national service will yield more benefits than an additional dollar spent on medical research, technological innovation, or any number of other private and public purposes. Indeed, the Clinton program will likely delay the entry of tens of thousands of people into the workforce every year, an economic impact that the President and his advisers appear not to have calculated. Yet the relative value of labor may rise in coming years as the population ages. As a result, the opportunity cost of diverting young people into extraneous educational pursuits and dubious social projects could rise sharply over time.

Another potentially important opportunity cost is diverting top quality men and women from the military. The end of the Cold War has sharply cut recruiting needs, but it also has reduced some of the allure of volunteering, as well as the perceived national need. As a result, by summer 1992 the Army, which typically has a more difficult recruiting task than the other services, was about 10% behind in signing up recruits for 1993. Observed General Jack Wheeler, head of the Army's recruiting effort, "I'm not panicking, but the numbers are disturbing." The military has even seen recruiting fall off in such traditional strongholds as northern Florida and other parts of the South. Various programs of educational benefit have always been an important vehicle for attracting college-capable youth into the military. Providing similar benefits for civilian service may hinder recruiting for what remains the most fundamental form of national service — defending the nation.

The military rightly fears the potential impact on a system that is working well. Observed Thomas Byrne of the private Association of the U.S. Army after the DLC proposal was unveiled, "We don't want high-caliber people who might otherwise join the Army off planting trees instead." The result, again, would be higher costs: economic, as more money would have to be spent to attract quality people; military, as the armed forces might become less capable; and moral, since military service would lose its preferred status, warranted by the uniqueness of the duties involved.

Still there are undoubtedly many worthwhile tasks nationwide that people could do. The problem in many cases, however, is that government effectively bars private provision of such services. Minimum-wage laws effectively forbid the hiring of dedicated but unskilled people and inhibit rehabilitation programs, like that run by the Salvation Army; restrictions on paratransit operations limit private transportation for the disabled. Licensing, zoning, and other unnecessary and often nonsensical regulations increase the price of day care. Similar sorts of restrictions harm private voluntarism as well. Health regulations prevent restaurants in Los Angeles and elsewhere from donating food to the hungry, for instance. In short, in many cases important needs are unmet precisely because of perverse government policy.

To the extent that serious problems remain, narrowly targeted responses are most likely to be effective. That is, it would be better to find a way to attract several thousand people to help care for the terminally ill than to lump that task with teaching, painting buildings, and a dozen other jobs to be solved by a force of hundreds of thousands. Talk of millions of "unmet social needs" is meaningless.

In any case, local organizations are not likely to efficiently use "free" labor from the federal government: staff members would have an almost irresistible temptation to assign hated grunge work rather than more suitable tasks to national servers. There are good reasons why many tasks that are not performed today are not performed, a fact ignored by national service advocates. In fact, a similar problem of perverse incentives has been evident in federal grant programs that allow states to use national money for projects without much local contribution. Observes David Luberoff of Harvard's John F. Kennedy School of Government, "One of the lessons of the interstate project is that in general . . . if you don't require that states put up a reasonable amount of the cost, you run the risk of building stuff that is probably not that cost-effective."

Real voluntarism, in contrast, works because the recipient organization needs to offer valuable enough work to attract well-motivated volunteers. But the Clinton program will simply assign people, people whose motivation would as likely be working off a school debt as "serving." In fact, the government risks subverting the volunteer spirit by paying loan recipients too much. The DLC suggested that its program promoted sacrifice, yet University of Rochester economist Walter Oi estimated that the total compensation − salary, health care benefits, and untaxed education/housing voucher − for "serving" was the equivalent of $17,500 annually after taxes, well above the mean earnings for high school graduates. The Clinton administration will offer compensation of at least $15,000 annually, and perhaps closer to $20,000, after including salary, health insurance, child care, and a tax-free education voucher. Such a wage won't make AmeriCorps participants rich, but it will make "service" a much better deal than, say, pumping gas. As a result, some students will likely see national service as a financially remunerative job option, not a unique opportunity to help the community.

Further, imagine the bureaucracy necessary to decide which 100,000 jobs are "service." Someone will have to sort through labor union objections to "unfair competition," match participants to individual posts, and monitor the quality of people's work. Can national service workers be fired? What if they refuse to do the work assigned to them? What if they show up irregularly or perform poorly? At what point does their legal right to the education voucher end?

Unwieldy Bureaucracy

These are not minor problems to be solved after the program is in place. To the contrary, the specifics go to the heart of the viability of any national service proposal. A Corporation for National and Community Service will make grants to states and local national service councils, and state governments will establish councils that will likely be composed of community groups along with local government officials, businessmen, and education and union representatives. These groups will hire staff, prepare plans, and oversee their implementation.

This sort of unwieldy bureaucracy is not likely to promote inexpensive and innovative solutions to human needs. Unfortunately, controls and regulations will inevitably follow federal labor and money. It is fear of just such consequences that has led the Guardian Angels, cited by national service advocate Charles Moskos as one of the most "striking examples of civic-minded youth volunteers," to reject federal grants. So does Habitat for Humanity, the Christian organization supported by former President Jimmy Carter that constructs housing for poor people.

Even worse, federal involvement is likely to politicize much of what is now private humanitarian activity. Members of Congress oppose efforts to close local government offices; interest groups lobby to twist social programs to their own benefit; labor unions mobilize to block proposals to contract out work. A program offering the free services of a hundred thousand young people will provide a massive honey pot attracting the worst sort of political infighting, with local and state officials demanding that "their" groups receive a "fair" share of the benefits.

Such battles could spill over into the courtroom. Religion pervades the volunteer sector; must churches and para-church groups eviscerate their religious focus in order to participate in the Clinton program? Equally problematic is the issue of controversial political, sexual, and social lobbies. One can imagine volunteers, backed by Democratic Party interest groups, wanting to treat work with Act-Up and Planned Parenthood as "service." The Clinton administration's attitude toward would-be volunteers at church day-care centers and non-liberal public interest groups like the National Taxpayers Union would likely be quite different. This returns to the basic questions: What is service? and Who decides?

The larger the federal program grows, the more cumbersome it is likely to become. Small programs under charismatic leaders, like the San Francisco Conservation Corps, have performed well; but their objectives are more limited, better defined, and more manageable. Moving from a few hundred to a hundred thousand is no easy task. Alas, the incredible fraud, misuse, and waste endemic to other "public service" programs, like CETA, hardly augur well for yet another, even larger, federal effort at social engineering.

In fact, CETA, with its system of federal funding for local jobs, is an important model. Aside from the nonsensical waste, reports policy analyst James Bovard, was the political abuse: "In Philadelphia, 33 Democratic party committeemen or their relatives were put on the CETA payroll. In Chicago, the Daley political machine required CETA job applicants to have referral letters from their ward committeemen and left applications without such referrals piled under tables in unopened mail sacks. In Washington, D.C., almost half of the City Council staff was on the CETA rolls." So awful was CETA that it became one of the few programs ever terminated by Congress.

Finally, money has to be an issue in a year when the President successfully pressed for massive tax hikes — three dollars for every dollar in spending cuts even by his own figures, and much more by more objective analyses. Unfortunately, national service will not come cheap. There will be more loans and thus more defaults, as well as the salaries and benefits paid to those who take government service jobs. The President acknowledged that his campaign program could more than double the cost of the current student loan program, between $4 billion and $5 billion, to some $12 billion. His more limited initiative, approved by Congress, will cost less; but the political dynamic of concentrated beneficiary groups versus the larger taxpaying public tends to promote the constant expansion of benefits once they are established. Even if the program eventually costs only an extra few billion dollars, it still will be difficult to justify spending so much money in this way, especially when the President just backed large-scale tax increases. Hiking expenditures so that private individuals can go to school for private gain is a dubious use of public money. And using national service to effectively hire 100,000 or more young people to do jobs of questionable worth is an even bigger waste.

Like the mythical Sirens, national service retains its allure. Argues Roger Landrum of Youth Service America, "Clinton has a shot at mobilizing the idealism and energy of a very significant number of young people, as Roosevelt did with the Civilian Conservation Corps and John F. Kennedy did with the Peace Corps." Alas, President Clinton's scheme is likely to end up no bargain. It probably will create a nightmarish bureaucracy and increase an already out-of-control deficit. National service also will reinforce today's misbegotten entitlement mentality, while siphoning tens of thousands of young people out of productive private labor and into make-work projects. Finally, if the program inflates tuition levels as student aid has done in the past, it probably won't even benefit many participants, since it will fund college administrators more than students.

What we need instead is a renewed commitment to individual service. People in community with one another need to help meet the many serious social problems that beset us. There is a role for government; officials should commit themselves to a strategy of "first, do no harm." We need to eliminate public programs that discourage personal independence and self-responsibility, that disrupt and destroy communities and families, and that hinder the attempts of people and groups to respond to problems around them. But the private activism that follows needs neither oversight nor subsidy from Big Brother. Some of the voluntarism can be part time and some full time; some can take place within the family, some within churches, and some within civic and community groups. Some may occur through profit-making ventures. The point is, there is no predetermined definition of service, pattern of appropriate involvement, set of "needs" to be met or tasks to be fulfilled. America's strength is its combination of humanitarian impulses, private association, and diversity. We need service, not "national" service. National service is an idea whose time will never come.

PART II
STUDENT LOANS

Student Loan Reform Act of 1993

By Madeleine M. Kunin

Madeleine May Kunin is the Deputy Secretary at the United States Department of Education. She works closely with Secretary Richard Riley on key education reform initiatives, including Goals 2000, School to Work, and Safe Schools legislation. She has taken the lead on reducing school violence and co-chairs the Clinton Administration's working group on violence prevention.

She served as Governor of the State of Vermont for three terms, from 1985 to 1991. After leaving office in 1991, Governor Kunin founded a nonprofit organization, the Institute for Sustainable Communities at Vermont Law School, to provide environmental assistance in Russia and Eastern and Central Europe. Governor Kunin was born in Zurich, Switzerland, and immigrated to the United States with her family in 1940.

At every stop along the presidential campaign trail, Bill Clinton was greeted with enthusiastic applause when he described his vision for national service and student loan reform. The proposal had resounding appeal for this new generation of young people, who sought an outlet for their desire to serve their country and relief from their worries about financing a college education.

President Clinton succeeded in fulfilling his campaign promises in his first seven months in office, through the enactment of the National Service Trust Act of 1993 and the Student Loan Reform Act of 1993. A further promise was kept to the American taxpayer when the Student Loan Reform Act was incorporated in the Omnibus Budget Reconciliation Act of 1993, where it will save $4.3 billion over five years.

The President envisioned a clear linkage between national service and student loan reform. If students could repay their loans as a percentage of their income, then student borrowers would be given the opportunity to take lower paying, service-oriented jobs while continuing to repay their debts.

Therefore, in the early stages, legislation for national service and student loan reform was developed jointly and expected to emerge as one piece of legislation. The Office of National Service in the White House and the Department of Education met frequently and often included representation from the Office of Management and Budget, Capitol Hill staff, the Internal Revenue Service, and the Council of Economic Advisers. As the Deputy Secretary of Education, I had been asked by Secretary Richard Riley to take the lead for the Department of Education; and Eli Siegel took the lead on behalf of the Office of National Service for the President.

Neither team had experience developing such complex and far-reaching legislation from the ground up. Therefore, we sought out expertise from many sources, building on the experience of the Congress and the career staff of the Department of Education. The usual turf boundaries between agencies were ignored as we developed practical and collegial working relationships, seeking advice and information wherever it seemed useful and appropriate. In addition, there were frequent outreach sessions with a broad spectrum of interest groups from the higher education and financial communities, which would be most directly affected by the legislation. From the start, we knew we were under an unusually urgent and abbreviated timeline to enable the President to introduce the joint bill in the spring. The Department of Education's determination to meet that deadline was motivated not only by the desire to adhere to the Administration's agenda, but also by the recognition that this was an opportunity for the Education Department to demonstrate its competence. Throughout the debate on direct lending, the ability of the department to be an effective manager was questioned by friend and foe alike.

Clearly, the first constituency we had to assure was our own, both within the Administration and among our supporters in the Congress. One benefit of our collegial working relationship in developing the legislation was that a basic level of trust in our competence was established, following a long period of friction and distrust in prior administrations.

In time it became apparent that the technical expertise demanded by direct lending and national service required separate meetings by the Department of Education and the Office of National Service. In addition, different political strategies were required for each half of the equation, both within the Congress and with separate constituencies.

Nevertheless, Eli Siegel and I continued to coordinate our efforts by telephone and meetings; and we jointly testified before the House. Our destinies converged again at a later stage, when the Congress raised concern about funding the Pell grant program and threatened to withhold support from national service until – and unless – funding for student financial aid was assured in the budget.

The decision to introduce separate companion bills was made by the White House shortly before sending the initiative to Congress on May 6. The inclusion of the Student Loan Reform Act in the Omnibus Budget Reconciliation Act was a significant factor in this strategy. National service would travel on another legislative route, following the regular authorization and appropriation process. The bifurcation of the two bills also was influenced by the more visible controversy surrounding student loan reform (in time, to be focused almost exclusively on direct lending), which was thought to slow down or even derail the national service bill. As it turned out, both pieces of legislation were enacted in close sequence: August 6 for direct lending and September 8 for national service.

However, the politics that worked for and against each legislative piece were vastly different. From the start, national service tapped into bipartisan public idealism and enjoyed strong congressional support, while student loan reform evoked a more partisan and polarized debate.

The enactment of national service would add a new program, thereby creating new winners; while direct lending would change an existing program, producing new winners *and* losers. National service was a straightforward program, with broad public appeal; direct lending was complex, an insider's game. The fact that national service cost money and direct lending saved money would play a significant role in the final analysis, slowing down national service and clinching the deal for direct lending; but in the early discussions, these cost savings were disputed.

Given the popularity of national service, it came as no surprise that when the bill was signed into law, it was under a wide white tent filled with music and fanfare on the White House lawn. When direct lending was signed into law, it was one of many footnotes to the Omnibus Budget Reconciliation Act of 1993, quickly lost in the happy celebration of the President's narrow deficit reduction victory.

The development of this presidential initiative from idea to reality, as well as its impact on public policy, is worthy of further exposition. The number of citizens directly affected by student loan reform is substantial: potentially almost 20 million students and their families, plus thousands of higher education administrators and employees of the lending community. The dollars involved − $4.3 billion in savings − are significant. And the underlying policy − providing better service at less cost − is central to the philosophy of the Clinton Administration.

Reforming the Student Loan Program: Why?

The day after Secretary Riley and I walked through the doors of the Department of Education on 21 January 1993, I discovered the December 1992 "high risk" report on student financial aid from the General Accounting Office on my desk. The sobering message was clear: student financial aid was in trouble, and the department's ability to manage it was in question.

The Federal Family Education Loan Program was "vulnerable to waste, fraud, abuse and mismanagement," the General Accounting Office concluded. Taxpayers were financing an expensive system at high cost with little accountability; the federal government was bearing almost all the risk of defaults and interest rate changes; and financial institutions were reaping the gains.

To its credit, the system provided millions of loans to students and their families each year. But the department clearly had to do better.

A subsequent briefing by GAO staff made it clear that with the present structure of 7,800 lenders, 46 guaranty agencies, and numerous servicers and secondary markets, the existing student loan system could not be fixed. We were not the first team to reach this conclusion. Numerous studies and congressional hearings over the years had indicated that the system needed major reform to introduce more accountability, reduce defaults, and achieve greater efficiency. In addition to creating unnecessary confusion and complexity, the existing system left borrowers with inflexible repayment options, preventing some students from accepting lower paying jobs and causing a greater number of loan defaults.

The problems that beset the student loan program highlighted a wonderful opportunity and also imposed a serious responsibility on the new Administration to prove that government could be "reinvented" to better serve its customers. The adage of Vice President Gore's reinvention report, while not yet coined, was already on our minds; we had a chance to develop an alternative that "worked better and cost less."

Simplifying the system by using direct loans rather than guaranteed loans, eliminating the middlemen and the excess profits they received, and shifting a percentage of those savings to students through lower fees and more flexible repayment options would provide better benefits to students and their families, reduce the administrative burden for colleges, and save taxpayers money. Such a window of opportunity is rarely opened in government.

The answer seemed obvious: Reform through direct lending would enable the Administration to keep its promise to both students and taxpayers. Who would argue with that conclusion?

In the next several months we would discover how the supporters and opponents of direct lending would debate these assumptions and forge a compromise that set the nation on a course toward direct lending and student loan reform.

The single most significant factor in making direct lending feasible was the Federal Credit Reform Act of 1990, which changed the scoring method, putting guaranteed and direct loans on equal footing. For the first time, credit reform looked at the subsidy costs of each program over the entire life of the loan. The new cost-savings figures that resulted gave a tremendous boost to the supporters of direct lending.

One of the first challenges facing the Administration was to establish agreed-on cost-savings numbers with the Department of Education, the Congressional Budget Office, and the Office of Management and Budget. At first there was considerable disparity among the various estimates, because different assumptions had been included in each; but at the end of March there was agreement that a savings of $4.3 billion would be achieved over five years with full implementation of direct lending. Included in the total savings were $2.5 billion needed for administrative costs to run the program.

That estimate never changed; only the timetable of implementing it was reconfigured. However, considerable confusion resulted when conflicting cost savings were floated, some of them introduced by opponents of the bill. The Congressional Budget Office was asked a "what if" question, to estimate cost savings using a different treatment of administrative costs than what was included in credit reform. That figure was $2.4 billion over five years. However, although this figure was widely used, it had no merit because savings had to be scored under the existing rules of the Federal Credit Reform Act.

A second challenge was to decide whether to adhere to the pilot direct lending program (authorized under the Higher Education Amendments of 1992), to expand on it, or to eliminate it and implement full direct lending, using the pilot as the first trial stage of full implementation.

Direct lending had been vigorously debated in 1992, but the final outcome was a small demonstration program that would have involved approximately $700 million in loan volume each year. This was a victory for opponents then, and now they continued to adhere to the same strategy. Why move forward toward direct lending, they asked, until we have the results of the pilot?

There were several problems with this approach, the major one being "time." It would take 5 to 10 years before the pilot provided significant answers, years that could be used to save money and to improve the program. In addition, there was the question of scope. The pilot was so small that it would tell us little about the economies of scale that would enable us to achieve cost efficiencies in a larger program. Finally, the specific design of the pilot was problematic.

After much debate, we concluded that the pilot program was too restrictive, but that the same goal of careful implementation could be achieved by a four-year phase-in of direct lending, giving the department the opportunity to self-correct *en route*.

Positive and Negative Factors Affecting Student Loan Reform

The President. The student loan reform debate changed significantly between 1992 and 1993 in large part because the Clinton Administration supported direct lending while the Bush Administration had opposed it. During the 1992 reauthorization of the Higher Education Act, the Bush Administration had threatened to veto the legislation if direct lending were included. However, some members of the Administration, including Charles Kolb and James Pinkerton of the domestic policy staff, had supported it even then and publicly declared their support in 1993.

The Congress. A group within the Congress had been staunch supporters of direct lending for many years, but their efforts had been thwarted because of opposition from the Administration. Their well-informed staffs were eager to work with new allies in the Administration. Senator Paul Simon and Congressman Robert Andrews were among those whose assistance was most beneficial at the outset.

As the legislation moved through the congressional process, the astute political skills and weighty influence of Chairman William Ford of the Committee on Education and Labor, and Senator Ted Kennedy, Chairman of the Labor and Human Resources Committee, were critical to its passage. Their close cooperation with the Administration, commitment to the bill's passage, and extraordinary success in achieving appropriate compromises enabled the legislation to pass.

Senator Kennedy's committee succeeded in winning the support of Senator Kassebaum and Senator Jeffords, resulting in a 15 to 2 bipartisan vote. Pivotal to the process was Senator Claiborne Pell, a skeptic of direct lending but a highly respected figure on student loans.

The key decision in both the House and the Senate was to score the $4.3 billion in the congressional budget resolution. Once that amount was part of the total budget savings, any critic of direct lending was obligated to find another source for $4.3 billion of savings — not a task easily achieved in an already highly contested budget process.

A critical vote took place on 24 March 1993, when Senator Nancy Kassebaum proposed an amendment in the budget resolution that would have reduced the savings to $3.4 billion. Five Democratic Senators voted in favor of the Kassebaum amendment, but the amendment was defeated 51 to 47. The good news was that the Administration's savings had prevailed. The troubling news was that Democratic support was not unanimous, indicating that the Administration had more work to do. In the House, the most vocal opponent of direct lending was Congressman Bart Gordon of Tennessee, who on several occasions demanded a direct vote on the question and wrote a number of letters of opposition to his colleagues.

In the Senate, serious questions were raised by Senator Sam Nunn, who had conducted an extensive review of student loan programs and brought these problems to our attention.

Prior to the House and Senate votes, the Department of Education — represented by then-Assistant Secretary-designate David Longanecker, Acting Assistant Secretary Maureen McLaughlin, and me — visited many members of Congress, including supporters, opponents, and those who were undecided. These personal visits not only allowed us to explain the bill, but also helped to establish the credibility of the department.

An important hearing was held by the Senate Labor and Human Resources Committee on May 25, where I and other members of the department had an opportunity to place ourselves on record in regard to our commitment to improving management in the Department of Education. For the first time, the department would undergo strategic planning, have an executive management committee, and engage a chief financial officer who was an overseer at GAO. The same emphasis was placed on management at the House hearings of the Committee on Governmental Operations.

The Department of Education. The most persistent question facing the department was its ability to manage. Therefore, the Secretary gave me the responsibility for management. Significant organizational and personnel changes began to establish faith in the department's competence, a prerequisite to gaining support for direct lending.

Emphasis on management improvement, however, would be an ongoing priority for the department. The greatest strength of the department was the level of expertise we discovered within the career staff, and our most significant success was to forge a close working relationship between the political and career members of the department. In early direct-lending discussions, skepticism was expressed about both the timetable and the concept by several people. However, as the circle of inclusion expanded, a team spirit developed; and those who would have to implement the law had a critical role in writing it.

Supporters. Almost all the associations representing students and institutions of higher education supported the Student Loan Reform Act because they saw the clear benefits that would accrue. In addition, because higher education was facing severe budgetary problems in many states, there was the hope that, as a result of these savings for the taxpayer, higher education might receive more favorable budgetary consideration in the future. The leaders of these associations were critical to counter-acting the adverse lobbying that was simultaneously being carried out by Sallie Mae and some members of the banking and guarantee agency community.

The Administration suffered from an early information disadvantage. We could not explain our program until the bill was in its final form and introduced. However, in the meantime, opponents could use their extensive resources to engage top-flight lobbying firms to bombard the higher education community with reports of the adverse effects that the opponents anticipated from direct lending.

Many of these opponents' assumptions were incorrect. For example, the cost of participating in direct lending was greatly inflated and aroused the concern of small schools and black colleges. However, the Administration did not have an opportunity to counter these charges until a later date, when an all-out effort was launched to provide accurate information about the bill and its impact. A summary of the information included in the departmental publication, "Myths and Realities," follows:

Myths and Realities

Myth — The cost savings attached to direct loans are overestimated because they do not accurately account for administrative costs. Moreover, they shift costs to the institutions for originating, servicing, and collecting student loans.

Reality — Direct lending saves money because the government has a lower cost of funds and excess profits are eliminated. In addition, our budget estimates include generous allowances for administrative costs as well as estimates of costs associated with the transition from guaranteed loans to direct loans. For institutions, the only new activities required under direct lending will be origination of loans and reconciliation of the amounts disbursed. Moreover, institutions will receive a fee from the Department of Education if they originate loans, and an alternative originator will be available at no cost for institutions that do not originate loans.

Myth — The Department of Education cannot manage the current system. A new, untried system will be even more difficult.

Reality — It is true that the department must strengthen its management capacities and the new Administration is investing heavily in management improvement. We must improve management regardless of whether we move to direct lending, however. This new, streamlined program will be easier to manage than the current complex system. It will build a new public/private partnership to select contractors, who will compete on the basis of price and quality, to act as alternative originators and to service loans. We have experience with a direct loan program, the Federal Perkins Loan program, and we know it works and that institutions can run it.

Myth — Institutions do not have the capacity to administer direct lending.

Reality — We know, based on experience, that many institutions can easily administer direct lending. Schools participating in current loan programs already determine eligibility, counsel students, and disburse loan funds. Schools participating in the Perkins Loan program already administer loans to students through their financial-aid offices. Moreover, direct lending will be easier than Perkins Loans, because schools will not be responsible for servicing or collecting loans.

Those institutions that do not have the capacity to administer loans will use the services of alternative originators at no cost. The Department of Education will monitor schools closely and will develop strict criteria, measuring their financial and administrative capacity to determine which schools can originate and which will be required to use the services of alternative originators. This will prevent unscrupulous schools from having greater access to federal funds and driving up default costs.

Our position was strengthened by reports from the Congressional Budget Office and the General Accounting Office that confirmed that direct lending would save substantial amounts of money compared to the existing system.

Early in the debate, it was clear that full implementation of direct lending had provoked a high-stakes debate. Healthy profits had been earned through the student loan program, and these profits would not be easily relinquished. The student loan portfolio, an Education Department study confirmed, was the third most profitable niche for banks, preceded only by credit cards and commercial and industrial loans.

And the earnings of Sallie Mae, a congressionally chartered, stockholder-owned corporation, were a matter of public record. The *Washington Post* had reported on January 13 that profits were up 19% in 1992 from 1991. The GAO reported that the Sallie Mae CEO earned $2.1 million and the top four administrators made at least $726,000 apiece.

The lobbying clout of the financial community, which stood to be adversely affected by direct lending, turned out to be more of a liability than an advantage. Contrary to the customary political dynamics of Washington, where the powerful usually prevail, in this case the powerful withdrew because their financial success could be interpreted as greed, which made members of Congress squeamish about any linkage between their interests and the banks and Sallie Mae.

No one who opposed direct lending did so in defense of these players. That is why management of the department became the only issue that could be debated; and the reduction of profits for the lenders and guarantee agencies became the strategy of opponents of direct lending, an unprecedented step for any interest group — to ask to receive less for its services.

At first this sacrifice of profits was believed capable of staving off the threat of direct lending. No one could recall when the banks had offered to reduce their earnings in prior debates. In fact, the reverse was true; any threat in that direction had aroused cries of insolvency and threatened the shortage of loan capital.

Therefore, the first victory of the Clinton Administration was achieved before passage of the bill, as banks agreed to reduce their profits. What was not anticipated, however, was that in the final version of the bill, the Congress would not choose between direct lending and reduced profits; it would do both. Only the timetable and the precise language would be contested, and that became the central focus of the compromise.

The event that placed the spotlight on lobbying efforts of the financial community and turned the tide in favor of direct lending was a May

25 news conference by Senator Paul Simon at which a student, Robert Kraig, testified that Sallie Mae had flown him and others to Washington to talk about setting up a student group to lobby against direct lending. The resulting headlines, which referred to "shady tactics," created greater distance between opponents of direct lending and the Congress, making the supporters' position more attractive.

Other Student Loan Reform Issues

The Role of the States. In early discussions, a state/federal partnership was envisioned that would enable states to become loan originators or contract out. Congressional staff and higher education groups strongly opposed that route, cognizant of the heated debate that had taken place the previous year in the reauthorization of the Higher Education Act. Despite the proclivity of the new education team for state involvement — mine as a former governor and David Longanecker's experience running a state commission on higher education — our allies in the Congress and the academic community were not comfortable with further state involvement. Therefore, the approach was dropped. It resurfaced in a more modest form during the final hour through an amendment by Senator Jeffords that asked the department to involve states if they could perform activities at a competitive price and quality.

Income Contingent Repayments. The proposed flexible repayment options — including income contingency — were accepted quickly and with rather limited debate. Two factors contributed to this.

First, the flexible repayment options represented a major benefit to students. Borrowers would be able to choose the repayment plan that best suited their needs and would be able to switch plans as their financial situations changed.

Second, direct lending diverted attention from the repayment side. Direct lending was a highly contentious issue where the interest groups would lose substantially; the repayment options did not go to their pocketbooks in the same way. The interest groups viewed the repayment options as a secondary issue.

Internal Revenue Service. The Clinton Administration believed that the IRS would be very helpful in servicing and collecting student loans. Exactly how to involve the IRS in the long run required more study to make a careful decision than was available as we were developing the legislation. At a minimum, however, it was essential that the IRS provide income information to the Department of Education to verify the incomes of those borrowers who choose income-contingent repayments. The Department of Education, jointly with the Treasury Department and IRS, is now completing a study on the most effective way to involve IRS in student loan collections.

Transition Period. Throughout our discussions there was great concern about ensuring access to the existing guaranteed student loan program, while the department geared up to run the new direct lending program. Access to loan capital and the viability of existing guarantee agencies remained concerns. Funds and strategies were included in the legislation to provide the Secretary of Education with the resources necessary to address problems during the transition.

Student Financial Aid Reform. While there was support for further reforming student aid programs to make them more effective, it was decided to postpone such reform legislation until the following year and concentrate on enforcement of existing law. Complicating this bill might jeopardize the timetable for its passage.

Final Compromise

The Student Loan Reform Act, as signed into law on 10 August 1993, allows the opposition some time to continue to make its case and thereby declare a measure of victory. But the outcome is clearly a success for the Administration, because it closely follows the President's proposed reform plan and, in some respects, exceeds it. For example, students will enjoy immediate cost savings in reduced fees and interest rates. The simplicity of the program also is anticipated to be advantageous to institutions of higher education. In addition, there will be new winners, compensating for many of the losers, as competitive contracts are awarded to carry out the law.

The major focus of debate in the conference committee was the timetable under which direct lending would be implemented and whether lending would exceed 50% before the Congress could re-evaluate the question. Some believed there should be two systems competing with one another. The Administration believed there had to be a commitment to going forward with direct lending; running two different programs over an indefinite period of time would place the department in an untenable managerial position.

The compromise language sped up implementation faster than anticipated in order to gain the cost savings: 5% the first year, 40% the second year, and as much volume as could be attracted in the third, fourth, and fifth years. Potentially, this enables the department to move toward full direct lending, if the program is attractive to students and institutions, without coercing participants.

The first round of 1,100 applicants was larger than anticipated, enabling the department to select a representative group of 105 institutions. The first direct loans will be made in the summer of 1994, and the second round of applicants will be selected in the spring.

While there was much debate about the advantages and disadvantages of direct lending as this legislation was developed and adopted, and critics will continue to scrutinize the department closely, there is agreement on all sides that the key to fulfilling the promise of direct lending rests with its implementation. The Administration is committed to achieving implementation in a timely and effective fashion. A reliable, cost efficient, and accessible system of student financial aid is essential to this generation of students and their families, who today, more than ever, look to higher education for a secure future.

The Direct Student Loan Program: Acknowledging the Future

By Congressman William D. Ford

Democrat William D. Ford has represented southeastern Michigan in the House since 1965. He was immediately assigned to the Committee on Education and Labor, where he helped write the federal government's initial education programs, including the Elementary and Secondary Education Act and the Higher Education Act. He became committee chairman in 1991. Having attended college and law school on the GI Bill — the first member of his family to go to college — he has remained determined that other Americans should have similar educational opportunities.

On 15 November 1993, 105 institutions of higher education were selected to participate in the first year of the Federal Direct Student Loan Program. These institutions were chosen from a field of more than 1,100 institutions that asked to participate. The very existence of this program shows President Clinton's and the Congress' commitment to change federal policy for the benefit of the taxpayer and the students who are recipients of federal programs. This program shows the President's commitment to overcome the forces of high-powered lobbying and special interest groups in Washington who chose to oppose the best opportunity to reinvent the student loan program.

The Federal Direct Student Loan Program provides a clear example of the education and economic policy differences between the current President and the former President. While President Clinton considers direct loans one of the foremost benefits of his 1993 economic reform package, President Bush threatened to brandish the veto pen when the $120 billion Higher Education Amendments of 1992 included a small direct loan pilot program. Why should such a simple program cause a political firestorm? First, I would like to clarify what the direct loan program entails.

What Are Direct Loans?

Under the existing federal student loan program, private capital from banks and other lending institutions is lent to students with the assistance of federal taxpayer support. This support comes in two forms: 1) the federal government ensures the lender a rate of return that covers the lender's cost of funds, administrative and servicing expenses, and a profit margin; 2) the federal government guarantees to repay the lender should the student borrower default.

If a student desires a federally guaranteed student loan, the student must meet the federally determined eligibility criteria and complete the Free Application for Federal Student Aid. The institution that the student is attending or desires to attend then certifies that the student is eligible for a loan and certifies the amount the student is eligible to borrow. The student takes this certification to a private lender to obtain a loan. Since most institutions of higher education have preferred lenders with which they do business, most students apply for the loan through the mail, without entering the doors of a bank.

The borrower begins repaying the loan six months after leaving the institution. There is a $50 minimum monthly payment and the borrower has 10 years to repay the loan.

In order to assist in the servicing and collection of these loans, a complex system of "middlemen" has developed to intervene between the borrower, the lender, and the government. Each state has a designated guaranty agency, which has the role of insuring the student loan made by the lender. The guaranty agencies are then reinsured by the federal government. There currently exist some 40 to 45 student loan secondary markets, including the Student Loan Marketing Association (a government-sponsored enterprise created as a student loan secondary market), which purchase student loans from lenders, providing these lenders with the liquidity to make more student loans. In addition, a number of loan servicers exist whose primary, if not sole business, is federal student loans. Lenders and secondary markets contract with these servicers to service and collect student loans.

Under the Federal Direct Student Loan Program, the federal government will provide capital directly to the schools, which will make the loans to the students. The federal government will be responsible for servicing and collecting these loans.

A far simpler model is triggered if a student desires a direct student loan. First, the student must meet the federally determined eligibility criteria and complete the Free Application for Federal Student Aid. Then the institution will provide the funding to the student. The federal government will contract with private agencies to service and collect the loans.

Why Direct Loans Are Attractive to the President and Congress

Direct loans are attractive for three basic reasons: 1) they save the federal taxpayer money; 2) they are simpler for the borrower, the school, and the Department of Education; and 3) they enable the federal government to provide alternate repayment options to the borrower.

First, holding administrative costs constant, direct loans are cheaper because the federal government's cost of funds is less than that of private lenders; and the federal government does not need a profit margin to induce it to make student loans. The Department of Education, the General Accounting Office, and the Congressional Budget Office all estimate that replacing the guaranteed student loan program with a direct loan program could save the taxpayers, at a minimum, $1 billion to $1.4 billion annually.

Second, the direct loan program will be infinitely simpler and less bureaucratic because it has one lender (the federal government) and a limited number of servicers (all under contract with the federal government) to substitute for the 7,500 to 8,000 lenders, about 90 guaranty agencies and secondary markets, and about 20 major servicers in the guaranteed program. This reflects the President's and Congress' commitment to reinvent government in order to simplify federal programs and eliminate federal bureaucracies or, as in this case, other bureaucracies that federal programs have created. Every additional agency that touches a student loan creates complexity for the borrower and the institution. Direct loans will ensure minimal involvement of the middlemen that serve only to complicate the student loan program.

It will be simpler for the borrowers because they will be able to obtain all of their student aid from the institution without the added step of going to a private lender. Also, under the current program, borrowers find that between the time they take out the loan and enter repayment, their loan has been sold, often more than once, or contracted out with a servicing agency. Under direct loans, all of a borrower's loans will be assigned to the same servicer, thus eliminating borrower confusion. Since all of the servicers will be under the same federal contract, there will be increased uniformity in policies and practices and, therefore, more equitable treatment for all students in the program.

103

Direct loans will be simpler for schools. Under the direct loan program, a school will estimate the need of its students for student loan funds and provide that estimate to the Department of Education. The department will forward loan funds to the school to disburse to its students. The school will then have a month or more after the beginning of classes to reconcile the funds received from the Department of Education with the funds paid to students. If the school does not want to originate these loans, the federal government will provide an alternate originator. This replaces a system where the school receives loan funds from a variety of lenders at different times and must disburse these funds to students. Schools that enroll students outside their state not only have to deal with multiple lenders and those lenders' forms and policies, but also with multiple guaranty agencies and their different forms and policies.

Direct loans also will be simpler for the Department of Education. Currently the department has oversight responsibility for 7,300 schools, 7,500 to 8,000 lenders, 46 guaranty agencies, 40 to 45 secondary markets, and 20 major servicers. Under direct loans, the middlemen will be eliminated. The department will need to oversee only the schools and the servicers with which the department contracts. This will help reduce the layers of red tape in the current student loan program. By reducing the number of program participants the federal government has to oversee, we have increased the ability of the federal government to do a good job in its oversight activities. This will help eliminate fraud and abuse in the federal student loan program. This move also echoes the Administration's calls to reinvent government by downsizing in order to promote quality.

The third major reason that direct loans are attractive to Congress is that they enable Congress to provide students with alternate repayment options. Under the current system, because a private lender owns the loan, any adjustments to the terms and conditions of the loan must yield the same profit. The borrower may not have an extended repayment period or an income-contingent repayment option without ensuring that the private lender will make the same, if not greater, profit on a student loan as on another investment. This is as it should be; private lenders need to make money for their owners.

However, the purpose of federal student-aid programs is to provide students with the ability to finance their college education. Grant funding has been decreasing and college costs have been rising during the past decade, and so students are graduating with unprecedented amounts of indebtedness. College education is supposed to equalize students by allowing graduates from lower- and upper-income backgrounds to compete for the same job. However, the College Board found that in comparing students ten years after college, those with student loan indebtedness had substantially lower assets than those earning the same amount with no student loan debts.

President Clinton recognized the problem of student loan debt by proposing alternate repayment schedules under the Federal Direct Student Loan program. Congress also enacted the President's legislation to allow students to cancel some of their loan debt through serving their community. Under the direct loan program, students will have the option of the standard 10-year repayment period, graduated repayment (smaller monthly payments at the beginning of the loan repayment period and increasing over time), extended repayment (allowing students more than 10 years to repay their loans, thereby reducing their monthly payment), income-contingent repayment (monthly payments as a percentage of the borrower's income), or a combination of these alternatives. This flexibility, which is possible because the federal government is the holder of the loan, will prevent defaults and will allow students to finance their education according to their individual needs.

Background of Direct Loans During the 102nd Congress

The idea of having the federal government directly provide the capital for student loans has been around for at least two decades. However, this concept was never seriously considered by Congress because of the way the cost of the program was calculated. The entire amount of the capital made available by the federal government was considered a "cost" to the government in the year in which the loan was made. In the following years, when the borrower began repaying the loan, this cost was offset. However, because Congress looks at the federal budget in five-year cycles (and the majority of the loan would not be collected during the first five years), a direct loan ended up looking like a grant on the federal budget tables. Therefore, direct loans had always implied tripling or quadrupling the cost of the program in the first year.

However, at the Bush Administration's recommendation, "Credit Reform" was adopted as part of the 1990 budget agreement. Under Credit Reform, the cost of direct loans is calculated as the "net present value" of the loans made in any one year. In other words, for budgetary purposes, the "cost" of the loans made in any year will be calculated as

105

the amount of capital made available, minus the anticipated future repayments of principal and interest, plus the future administrative and default costs. Using this method of determining costs, direct loans became not only competitive with guaranteed loans on a cost basis but, as previously noted, substantially cheaper for the taxpayer.

Credit Reform was enacted at the very end of the 101st Congress. During the 102nd Congress, the Higher Education Act was scheduled for reauthorization. This is a process Congress undertakes every five years to examine federal student financial assistance and other higher education programs to determine what changes are necessary in order to reflect the current needs of students and institutions.

In the first months of 1991, Congress asked the Administration and the higher education community to think about possible revisions to the Higher Education Act. The Administration was among the first to float a major proposed change.

On 7 January 1991, The *New York Times* published an article, titled "U.S. May Alter Student Lending to Skirt Banks," reporting that "the Bush Administration is considering major changes in the student loan program that would increase direct lending by the federal government and sharply curtail the role of commercial banks." The *Washington Post*, on 8 January 1991, reported that the "White House is reviewing the proposal for possible inclusion in President Bush's 1992 budget request and his legislation on reauthorizing higher education programs." The *New York Times* stated that the savings generated by this conversion "could then be used to provide more aid to the neediest college students, in keeping with Mr. Bush's pledge to be 'the education President,' Administration officials said."

These press reports encouraged the higher education community, both the colleges and the lenders, to examine seriously the effects of a transition from a guaranteed student loan program to a direct loan program.

Congress had already agreed that this reauthorization was going to be comprehensive, examining all of the higher education programs to see if they were still effective. I did not want the 1992 reauthorization to be a repeat of the 1981 or 1986 reauthorizations during the Reagan years. During both of those reauthorizations, budget constraints allowed Congress only to tinker around the edges of the programs, without the opportunity to examine any significant changes. At the beginning of the 101st Congress, both House and Senate committees expressed enthusiasm for considering new ideas in higher education, including direct lending.

106

During April and May of 1991, the higher education community and the Department of Education submitted their recommendations for reauthorization. The American Council on Education (ACE), the umbrella organization that represents college presidents from all sectors of higher education (four-year and two-year, public and private), proposed establishing a direct student loan program. ACE proposed to use the savings generated from this program to raise student's loan limits and to reduce student's loan fees.

When Secretary of Education Lamar Alexander testified before the House Subcommittee on Postsecondary Education, I observed that the Administration's testimony on the reauthorization of the Higher Education Act did not specifically mention direct loans. The Secretary responded that the department was not actively considering direct loans. He testified that their first priority was to control the current programs. He said that the department's second priority was to "look quickly and carefully to see if there are alternate ways of managing this big enterprise in a way that would save money and improve services. When we get to that, of course, we will consider the direct loan idea."

At that hearing, I also asked the Secretary for the Department of Education's analysis on the direct loan program and potential savings. Two months later I finally received the data, which showed federal savings estimated at $1 billion to $1.4 billion annually as a result of converting to a direct loan program.

About the same time as the Secretary testified before the House, a study titled "Lender Profitability in the Student Loan Program," which had been prepared for the Department of Education, was released. In the executive summary, the report concluded, "This study demonstrates that student lending has been a consistently profitable activity for lenders. Moreover, it is shown that student lending has generally been more profitable than other important lending activities such as mortgage and automobile lending. The relatively high level of student loan profitability is due to their guaranteed yield, as well as their low level of credit and liquidity risk. The profitability of student lending is also found to have less variability when compared to other types of bank lending." This study helped fuel the discussion on the feasibility of direct lending.

The Subcommittee on Postsecondary Education conducted 44 hearings during the period from 18 March through 1 August 1991. Most of these hearings were held in Washington; however, 19 of them were held across the country. Twenty-four witnesses at 13 different hearings testified on direct loans. On 12 June 1991, the subcommittee devoted most of one hearing to the examination of direct loans.

Members of the House and Senate also introduced legislation on direct loans. Congressman Petri from Wisconsin, a long-time advocate of income-dependent loan repayment, introduced legislation to convert to a system of direct loans to establish this repayment mechanism for all borrowers. Congressman Miller of California and Senator Simon also introduced legislation to convert to a system of direct loans to allow borrowers to have an income-sensitive repayment schedule. Congressman Andrews of New Jersey introduced legislation to transition from the guaranteed loan program to a system of direct lending, using the savings generated to provide borrowers with lower loan fees and higher loan limits. When the subcommittee began to draft legislation to reauthorize the Higher Education Act, we had the benefit of an expansive and thorough hearing record on the issue of direct lending, as well as many legislative proposals.

What the 102nd Congress Sent to the President

In developing a proposal for the reauthorization, the Subcommittee on Postsecondary Education decided to include a phase-in of direct lending modeled on the legislation introduced by Congressman Andrews. The committee's proposal used the savings generated from this transition to increase students' loan limits, reduce student loan fees, and finally to ensure adequate funding for the Pell grant program by converting it to an entitlement.

This is the one provision in the reauthorization on which the subcommittee and the Education and Labor Committee split along party lines. The Democrats on the committee supported a Pell grant entitlement and a phase-in of direct lending. The Republicans, in general, opposed both concepts. The committee began consideration of H.R. 3553, the Higher Education Amendments of 1992, on 22 October 1991, and approved the bill on 23 October 1991.

Since testifying before the subcommittee in May, the Administration also had changed its position on direct loans. On 21 October 1991, Secretary Alexander wrote me saying, "If the bill were presented to the President with either the Pell grant entitlement or a Direct Loan replacement for the Guaranteed Student Loan Programs, the President's senior advisors would recommend that he veto the bill." What had started in January as an Administration proposal was veto bait by October.

Over the next few months, the House committee leadership was faced with the Administration's veto threat; broad opposition from House Republicans; antagonism from lenders, guaranty agencies, and secondary markets; and the anxiety of many colleges about the prospect of a dramatic change in the student loan program. To smooth the path of the reauthorization on the House floor, and in recognition that a presidential veto would threaten the ability of millions of students to attend college in the fall, it was agreed to back off a full transition into direct lending and include only a pilot program as part of the reauthorization. This direct loan pilot program was incorporated into the committee substitute, along with the elimination of the Pell grant entitlement. This compromise passed the House by an overwhelming margin. However, the Statement of Administration Policy still recommended that the President veto this bill, largely because of the inclusion of the direct loan pilot program.

Despite some support for direct loans, the Senate committee was more impressed by the uncertainties rather than the promise of direct loans and did not include any version of direct loans in its reauthorization bill.

There were more than 1,500 specific items of disagreement between the House and Senate bills, many of them much more substantive than direct loans. However, the Administration decided to focus its attention on the existence of a direct loan pilot program. The Senate agreed to accept a direct loan pilot program. Within minutes of the end of the conference, Secretary Alexander released a press statement charging that the direct loan pilot program "destroyed" the bill and stated that "President Bush should veto this legislation."

It took a group of Republican members of the House Education and Labor Committee meeting personally with the President to convince him that it was not politically prudent for the "education President" to veto a major piece of education legislation that would expand student aid to hundreds of thousands of middle-income families, on the grounds that a pilot program that saved federal taxpayers' dollars was a little "too big." I view this politically based insensitivity to students' needs as a defining difference between the past and current Administrations.

The 1993 Budget Reconciliation

An unanticipated door was opened soon after the Clinton Administration began the arduous task of transition into office. As their education representatives began consulting with congressional members and staff about the primary issues confronting the 103rd Congress, there was an opportunity to explain in greater detail the ramifications of the direct loan program.

It was obvious from the campaign that the President was predisposed to pursuing new and innovative ways of assisting students and making

109

postsecondary education an affordable and attainable goal. The attractiveness of the direct loan program to the incoming Administration was multiplied by the federal budget savings associated with it. As I previously noted, the range of estimates by the varying bean counters in town pointed to a $1 billion to $1.4 billion savings per year once the program was up and running.

The budget reconciliation process that greeted both the new Administration and the newly elected 103rd Congress set the table for a renewed effort to take the next step in the direct loan program's maturation process. The official process of finalizing the President's budget and marrying the needed revenues and savings is a complicated one that cuts across all departments and jurisdictions in both the executive and legislative branches of government. The President put together a package of programmatic savings and revenues that amounted to a target of $500 billion over five years. Of that total, $4.6 billion in programmatic savings were required from the postsecondary education programs over which my committee has jurisdiction.

As stated in his "Vision for Change in America" speech to the nation, the President and his newly appointed Secretary of Education, Governor Richard Riley, proposed to achieve this savings by embracing the direct loan program as a top programmatic priority in the President's budget.

I had strong support from my Democratic colleagues on the Education and Labor Committee. They had joined me in the previous Congress in supporting the proposed changes associated with a direct loan program and were already well-versed in the pros and cons associated with the program.

On the Republican side I was joined in support of the transition by Congressman Petri. The ranking member of the full Committee, Congressman William Goodling of Pennsylvania, opposed the move to full implementation of the direct loan program. He voiced his concerns about the lack of assurance that the system could succeed, given the management limitations of the existing Department of Education. He voiced his strong support for staying the course on the pilot direct loan program so that we could see if the idea was sound and see if the department was up to the task.

I have great respect for my colleague from Pennsylvania and am proud of the work we have done together on the committee. On education matters we normally are walking side-by-side and not so diametrically opposed. But in this case we simply have differing views of what is needed for our nation's students and what changes are needed to ensure continued access to quality postsecondary educational opportunities.

I have been very impressed by the new spirit and commitment that is taking control in the Department of Education. After 12 years of the department being targeted for either elimination or dramatic program cuts, we have entered an era of renewed importance for the department's issues and goals. Rather than simply saying that one wanted to be the "education president," it takes action to merit the title. The high priority that the direct loan program received from the new Administration succeeded in raising not only the expectations for the department but the prestige as well.

Despite Congressman Goodling's concerns, which were shared by members on both sides of the aisle, we moved forward with the programmatic changes; and in May 1993 we reported out of committee the programmatic changes needed to accomplish the savings charged to our committee.

Because of the savings requirement, the committee was faced with the choice of a transition to direct lending or drastic cuts in profits to lenders in the guaranteed program. However, the way we ensure access in the guaranteed program is by paying lenders to make these loans. The lending community has been telling Congress for 15 years that any cuts in their profits will result in fewer loans to students. Therefore, the committee reported out the bill that the President sent to Congress with few modifications. The legislation provided for a five-year transition from the current guaranteed loan program to a direct loan program. The bill included a variety of alternate repayment options for students. The legislation included necessary authority for the Department of Education to manage the transition from guaranteed loans. The committee bill also provided reduced interest rates and lower loan fees to students.

The debate over the budget took on a national dynamic that eclipsed all discussion of the direct loan program. The reality was that the focus of the debate turned to the total savings the reconciliation process had to derive, as opposed to the programmatic changes represented by the direct loan program.

As the normal legislative process was moving forward, the lending community's opposition to the direct loan program was building. Despite the fact that our language allowed the lenders to continue for five years to receive the same premiums and profits on loans they process, they did not feel a phase-in to direct lending was necessary. The bankers would have $83.5 billion in loans to service at the end of the transition.

These loans would not be totally paid off until 2015. During the transition, lenders would receive between $2.5 billion and $3 billion annually in subsidy costs.

The lobbying pressure that the members of my committee experienced at this time was far different from any they had received on issues before the committee at any other time. Direct loans attracted the same kind of lobbying attention that Ways and Means Committee issues usually receive. This resulted in letters and other communications to committee members, the Secretary of Education, and the President, demanding a rejection of the 100% phase-in to direct loans and a continuation of the status quo.

Despite these distractions, the House continued to move ahead and included the 100% phase-in to direct lending in the House-passed budget reconciliation bill, H.R. 2264, in May 1993.

This action set the stage for the conference between the House and the Senate in July 1993. Both were charged with finding the savings, but we took very different approaches. By moving to the 100% phase-in over four years, the House accomplished the required savings in a much cleaner and less destabilizing manner than our Senate counterparts. As I stated earlier, we thought it best to keep the profits generating from the program to the lending community whole and untouched for the entire phase-in period. This seemed to be the least intrusive method for change. In addition, it was shown that during the phase-in, the lending community would have continued to generate loans that would have remained in repayment till 2015.

At this point I want it to be clear that I am grateful to the private lending community for their work with the committee and the student loan programs. But this program was not created to assist lenders; it was created to ensure students access to equitable funding for higher education. I feel confident that the lending community understands this fact, as does the Congress.

The House and Senate conferees worked long and hard to achieve an agreement that was satisfactory to both the House and the Senate. The final conference agreement provided for a transition from the guaranteed student loan program to a direct loan program beginning in the 1994-95 academic year. This transition is not mandatory, as in the House-passed bill; rather, it is voluntary, allowing any institution that desires to participate in the direct loan program to do so beginning in the 1996-97 academic year. The compromise requires that at least 60% of the student loan volume be made under the direct loan program by the 1998-99 academic year.

Because the transition is not mandatory, cuts in lender profits and guaranty agency and secondary market revenues were necessary in order to achieve the savings mandated by the budget resolution. However, the conference agreement contained provisions to ensure that students will have access to loans during the 1994-95 and 1995-96 academic years, when the direct loan program will be capped. The Department of Education has the authority to advance funds to guaranty agencies to serve as lenders-of-last-resort for students or to require the Student Loan Marketing Association to act in this capacity. The conferees were committed to providing students with the same interest rate benefits and loan fee reductions that were contained in the House and Senate bills.

Congress is committed to monitoring this transition closely to ensure that students have access to student loan funds and that the savings targets are achieved. As the program evolves, changes must be made to ensure that the taxpayers' funds are efficiently handled and that we are taking advantage of every cost-saving technique available. More efficient and effective government is what this change represents.

The Federal Direct Student Loan Program is a tremendous opportunity for this Administration and its Department of Education to demonstrate what President Clinton's vision for change in America encompasses. This program shows a sharp contrast between the policy priorities of the Bush and Clinton presidencies. This program also shows that it is possible to reduce federal spending, to streamline federal bureaucracy, to simplify a federal entitlement, and to offer better service and benefits to the students this program was designed to assist. While this will be a great challenge for the President and his Department of Education, I am proud to have been part of the congressional process that had the courage to give the President this opportunity.

Direct Student Loans: A Questionable Public Policy Decision

By Congressman Bill Goodling

Congressman Bill Goodling represents the 19th District in Pennsylvania. Following military service in the late 1940s, Goodling earned a bachelor's degree from the University of Maryland, a master's degree in education from Western Maryland College, and completed coursework toward a doctoral degree from Pennsylvania State University.

He worked as a teacher and principal and, beginning in 1967, served as superintendent of schools for the Spring Grove Area School District in Pennsylvania before being elected to Congress in 1974. Goodling represents Adams, Cumberland, and York Counties in south-central Pennsylvania.

In 1993, Congress mandated a fundamental change in the method for providing federal student loans. Prior to 1993, the primary vehicle for providing federal student aid was through the guaranteed student loan program. Under this program, federal student loans were made and serviced by the private sector but were guaranteed and subsidized by the federal government. As part of the 1993 congressional budget resolution and reconciliation, Congress adopted a Clinton Administration proposal that directed the U.S. Department of Education to begin to replace the Guaranteed Student Loan (GSL) program with a direct loan program under Public Law 103-66. Although touted by its supporters as a measure that would save money and simplify the loan program, direct loans are not likely to do either. The savings and increased efficiencies that supposedly will be realized by direct lending are illusory. They are based on unrealistic assumptions and, therefore, are unlikely to accomplish their objectives.

Guaranteed Loans

The primary source of federal aid to postsecondary students is through federal student loans — about $18 billion in loans were made to more than 5.7 million students in FY 93 (U.S. Department of Education, 1993). Before passage of the Clinton direct loan program, the principal vehicle for delivery of federally subsidized student loans was the GSL program, which had been renamed the Federal Family Education Loan Program in the 1992 Amendments to the Higher Education Act. (For the purposes of this essay, I will use GSL to refer to the program both before and after the amendments.) Under the GSL program, loans are made with private capital, while the government ensures the lender a return that covers all of the lender's costs and guarantees the lender a profit margin. If a student becomes delinquent, the lender attempts to collect what is owed. If the lender cannot collect the loan within a prescribed period, a guaranty agency — established or designated by each state to monitor school and lender compliance — reimburses the lender for the defaulted amount and attempts to collect that amount from the borrower. If the guaranty agency cannot get the loan into repayment, it turns the loan over to the Department of Education, which then tries to recover the money.

The GSL program was created by the Higher Education Act of 1965 as a means to ensure that no one would be denied access to postsecondary education because they lacked resources or sufficient collateral to secure a loan. In its 28-year history, the GSL program has provided financial support to many college students and their parents. Currently, the federal government, more than 7,800 financial institutions, 45 secondary markets including the Student Loan Marketing Association (Sallie Mae),* 46 guaranty agencies, dozens of loan servicers, collection agencies, and other service providers join together to deliver student loans. Not surprisingly, like any large federal program, the GSL program has developed into a complex system replete with successes and failures.

From the 1970s to mid-1980s, Congress attempted to promote educational opportunity for all students by greatly expanding eligibility for guaranteed student loans and by allowing proprietary schools to partic-

---

*The Student Loan Marketing Association, known as Sallie Mae, is the largest student loan secondary market in the nation. It is a stockholder-owned company that was created by the government in 1972 to ensure liquidity in the student loan market. As of 30 September 1993, Sallie Mae held $23 billion of the approximately $68.7 billion in outstanding guaranteed loans.

ipate fully in the GSL program. This effort was very successful and provided hundreds of thousands of adult learners, displaced homemakers, and others with access to new educational opportunities.

Unfortunately, during the same period, the Department of Education sharply reduced its audit and program review staff, allowing schools whose sole intention was to take advantage of federal funds to enter the program. These unscrupulous "schools" prospered at the expense of the American taxpayer and the GSL program. As a result, while default rates have remained relatively constant because of the influx of newly eligible schools, there was a dramatic increase in the volume of defaults under the GSL program. Widespread concern about abuse in the loan programs along with the increase in default volume spawned a variety of reform legislation in the late 1980s and early 1990s. As a consequence, a significant portion of the 1992 Higher Education Amendments was devoted to improving the integrity of the GSL program. (See Public Law 102-325, Title IV, Part H.)

These reforms already have paid off. Since 1992, the volume of defaults has begun to decline. For example, in 1981 the government paid off $257 million in defaulted student loans. By 1991, defaults had peaked at $3.2 billion; but in 1992 the default rate declined to $2.6 billion and is expected to decline further.

As congressional interest in student loan reform increased, members were divided between those who had positive experiences with the GSL program and those whose experiences were negative. The guaranty agency in my home state, the Pennsylvania Higher Education Assistance Agency, has an exceptional record of serving students and schools. As a consequence, there was no political pressure in Pennsylvania to replace the GSL program. In other states, the GSL program has gotten a mixed reaction and is seen as a complex program prone to fraud and abuse.

Direct Loans

As its name suggests, the direct loan program provides capital directly to schools, which in turn make loans to students. As a consequence, the financial intermediaries that are an indispensable component of the guaranteed program — lenders, secondary markets, and guaranty agencies — play no role in a direct loan program.

President Clinton offered two fundamental reasons for his decision to propose a switch to direct lending. First, he argued that significant cost savings could be achieved if the government made loans directly

117

to students. Second, direct lending would be made part and parcel of the President's efforts with his national service plan to provide borrowers with new options for student loan repayment. The direct loan program would be structured to give student loan borrowers an opportunity to gradually repay their loans through the Internal Revenue Service (IRS), based on a graduated percentage of future income.

The President's proposal to make wholesale changes to the federal student loan programs came to a Congress weary of debating the merits of federal direct student loans. Just four months prior to Mr. Clinton's election, Congress had completed work on the Higher Education Amendments of 1992. For the nearly two years that Congress considered this legislation, a long and heated debate raged over whether the GSL program should be supplanted by direct lending.

The Clinton proposal would have required significant revisions to existing federal law to authorize the IRS to collect student loan payments. The IRS historically has opposed becoming involved in student loan collections, because of the inherent complexity of these loans and, more important, the threat to the voluntary nature of the tax collection system posed by encumbering it with a debt collection system. In addition, a number of private organizations, including student groups, have questioned the appropriateness of exposing students to IRS collection techniques.

The introduction of direct lending into the debate on the 1992 amendments can be traced back to the Bush Administration. In early 1991, in developing its FY 92 budget and legislation reauthorizing the Higher Education Act, some high-ranking officials within the Administration suggested replacing the GSL program with a direct loan program as a cost-saving and program-simplification measure. This proposal ultimately was rejected by the Bush White House because of concerns that the Department of Education was ill-equipped to administer the program and that it would require massive federal borrowing. However, stories were leaked to the press that the concept had been under discussion and the proposal took on a life of its own ("Administration Seeking to Bypass Banks in Student Loan Program" 1991).

Congressman Robert Andrews (D-N.J.) introduced a bill in the summer of 1991 to completely phase out the GSL program and replace it with a direct loan program. In October 1991, the reauthorization bill, as reported from the House Education and Labor Committee, incorporated Congressman Andrews' bill. The Bush Administration and most House Republicans were adamantly opposed to the Andrews proposal.

They believed that: 1) the savings from direct lending were vastly over-stated, 2) direct loans would require the federal government to shoulder all of the default risk, 3) the Department of Education was not capable of administering the program, 4) massive amounts of federal borrowing would be incurred, and 5) many schools could not handle the responsibility of originating loans. President Bush threatened to veto the final reauthorization bill if it contained full-scale implementation of direct lending.

In the face of a veto threat and strong resistance from nearly all House Republicans (as well as some Democrats), the House committee leadership agreed to scale back direct lending to a pilot program prior to the proposal reaching the House floor. This decision was fueled by an aggressive lobbying effort against direct loans by lenders, secondary markets, and guaranty agencies.

In the Senate, the direct loan proposal enjoyed some support but not enough to include any provision for direct lending in the final Senate version of the bill. Senate support for direct lending focused on a direct loan program that relied on income-contingent repayment, which is discussed below. The House-Senate conferees on the 1992 Higher Education Amendments initially agreed to a demonstration project that would have allowed 500 institutions to participate with estimated annual lending in the $1 billion to $1.5 billion range.

The Bush Administration objected to the size of the pilot and once again threatened to veto the legislation. The House Republicans on the conference committee, who felt that it would be politically unwise to veto the bill, brokered a compromise between the Democrat conferees and the Bush Administration. The final legislation included a scaled-back demonstration project that was limited to a cohort of schools whose annual loan volume (for the most recent year data was available) did not exceed $500 million, thereby allowing only a limited number of postsecondary institutions into the program. The final legislation also included a modest experiment in the use of more flexible repayment options, including the use of income-contingent repayment.*

---

*During the debate on the 1992 amendments, Congressman Thomas Petri (R-Wis.), a longtime advocate of income-contingent repayment, joined with a bipartisan coalition, including Senators Bill Bradley (D-N.J.), Paul Simon (D-Ill.), and David Durenberger (R-Minn.), and Representatives George Miller (D-Calif.) and Sam Gejedson (D-Conn.), to push for direct lending and the inclusion of income-contingent repayment. Their efforts resulted in the inclusion of options for some borrowers to repay through the IRS on an income-contingent basis and created a new program for defaulted borrowers also to begin repayment through the IRS.

Policy Issues

As Congress considered direct lending in both 1992 and 1993, Republican members, myself included, repeatedly tried to debate the policy issues surrounding direct lending. These efforts were never fully successful. The final results of the legislation reflect more the politics of the Clinton Administration and the Democratic leadership than the substance of the issues. A review of the policy questions raised by direct lending reflects how key issues failed to be considered carefully in the final legislation enacted by Congress. The proponents of direct lending argue that direct lending saves money and is simpler to administer and more efficient than the guaranteed program. An examination of these arguments, as well as other issues, further raises many doubts about the advantages of direct lending over guaranteed loans.

Will direct loans save the taxpayers money? The primary argument in favor of direct lending is that it will save the government billions of dollars as compared to the guaranteed program. Direct loan advocates estimated that their proposal would save anywhere from $620 million to $1.5 billion, depending on specific program parameters.

In September 1991, the General Accounting Office (GAO) issued a report titled, "Student Loans: Direct Loans Could Save Money and Simplify Program Administration" (GAO/HRD-91-144BR). This report stated that the federal government could save between $620 million and $1.5 billion annually by moving from guaranteed to direct student loans. However, the GAO advised that its analysis needed to be viewed with caution, as it did not consider all of the federal expenditures associated with direct lending.

In November 1992, the GAO issued a more definitive report to Congress titled, "Direct Loans Could Save Billions in First Five Years with Proper Implementation." According to this report, a switch to direct lending could save the federal government about $4.8 billion in the first five years of implementation. These savings were attributed to the elimination of subsidies to banks, secondary markets, and other program participants. Serious questions remain about whether these savings will materialize on full implementation of direct lending.

The concept of the federal government providing the capital for student loans has been around for decades, but it had always been rejected as too costly. This was because the cost of capital made available by the government was considered a "cost" to the government in the year in which the loans were made. The rest is offset only gradually in future years as students repay their loans. Therefore, direct loans had always

120

cause the increase must be applied to all of the debt issued by the government — including all debt that finances the deficit, as well as debt that refinances the expiring debt — even very small increases in interest rates will effectively wipe out the savings claimed for direct lending. An increase in rates of two percentage points for each additional $10 billion of public debt issued will convert the move to direct lending from a deficit reduction measure to one that increases the government deficit (Penner 1993).

Can the Department of Education effectively administer a direct loan program? Much of the debate over direct lending centered on the Department of Education's ability to effectively manage a massive direct lending program. The tasks associated with direct lending will require the department to incur new staffing and administrative responsibilities at a time when there is broad agreement that it is only barely able to manage its existing program responsibilities.

A December 1992 GAO report to the then-incoming Clinton Administration directly addressed the issue of the department's lack of administrative capability, noting that "the inventory of known problems in the department's administration of the guaranteed student loan programs raises questions about its ability to adequately manage a direct lending program" (General Accounting Office 1992). More important, the report raised questions about whether the department was properly managing its existing program responsibilities. The GAO observed that the Department of Education "lacks proper systems and controls to adequately manage its multibillion dollar student assistance programs and problems erupting from these programs could eventually overwhelm any potential reform measures."

These concerns were consistent with the department's demonstrated failure to operate a program of direct loan guarantees when it attempted to do so in the 1970s. The Federally Insured Student Loan (FISL) program was directly administered by the department's predecessor, the Department of Health, Education and Welfare (HEW). HEW's administration of the program was characterized by numerous school closings, trade school rip-offs, students failing to receive loan checks, and similar problems. Based in part on these mistakes, Congress began phasing out the FISL program in favor of the GSL program as part of the 1976 reauthorization of the Higher Education Act.

Will direct lending lower the default rate? Student loan defaults are one of the most significant problems in the student-aid program. Defaults are the program's greatest federal cost. In FY 93, defaults cost the program approximately $2.5 billion.

In calculating the cost savings under direct lending, both GAO and CBO reports assume that the default rate will remain unchanged under direct lending. There is no indication that direct lending will have a positive effect on the default problem, while there is much that points to the possibility that direct lending could actually increase default rates as a result of borrower confusion. Because borrowers will receive both grant and loan aid from their institutions, they may be confused over which are loans and which are grants.

Furthermore, under the GSL program, guaranty agencies and lenders monitor default rates at all institutions and are able to identify problem schools by limiting the potential for excessive abuse of the program. This important control function will be lost under direct lending, since all the administrative responsibility for the loan would shift to a department that repeatedly has been faulted for its inability to screen bad schools out of the loan program.

Can all postsecondary educational institutions manage the increased responsibility inherent in direct lending? Many institutions are opposed to direct lending because they may not be able to absorb the added administrative responsibilities and costs that direct lending will entail. Some institutions also are concerned that the federal assistance promised under direct lending to help offset some of the administrative costs might disappear in future budget reconciliations, and that future federal belt-tightening might result in the imposition of institutional risk sharing.

The institutions in favor of direct lending generally fall into two categories: 1) institutions with large staffs and administrative capabilities and 2) private career schools. Because of their historically high default rates, these latter schools traditionally have had difficulty obtaining loan access in the GSL program; under direct loans they would access funds directly from the federal government.

A recent random survey of postsecondary institutions by the College Board found that institutions voiced three principal concerns. First, financial-aid administrators worried that political commitment to direct lending will not be sufficient to meet the long-term capital needs of the program. Second, there was the near-unanimous concern about the ability of the Department of Education to administer direct lending. Third, there was concern about schools' ability to absorb a new program into their already strained operations, in addition to concern about their exposure to liability under direct lending (College Board 1993).

Will the government be able to perform the administrative functions associated with running a loan program as efficiently as the private sector? As noted earlier, under direct lending the federal government will replace several thousand lenders, several dozen guaranty agencies, and the entire student loan secondary market. The CRS report concluded that because direct lending is not functionally simpler than the GSL program, budget savings can result only if the federal government has been over-paying the private sector for these services and the government can perform them at a lower cost.

The private sector has steadily reduced costs per loan over the last dozen years, largely because of technical innovations and the effects of competition in the loan servicing market. There is no empirical basis for believing that the federal government can provide these services at lower cost than the private sector. The simplicity achieved by ridding the program of multiple suppliers is not, in an economic sense, necessarily consistent with administrative efficiencies that reduce costs and produce budget savings. Cost savings are more likely to be generated by a structure that maintains competition at each level of the loan production process (Miles and Zimmerman 1993).

Political Issues

As noted previously, there are serious policy questions about direct lending that, because of political considerations, were not fully aired before the program was enacted. Unfortunately, these political issues became increasingly acrimonious and blocked meaningful debate on the merits of the direct lending proposal.

Direct loan proponents argued that the private sector participants were making "excess profits" at the expense of the government and students. Lenders, guaranty agencies, and secondary markets were viewed as the enemy. Not surprisingly, their efforts to defend the guaranteed program were ascribed to self-preservation and greed. Sallie Mae CEO Lawrence Hough's annual compensation package of nearly $2 million and Sallie Mae's healthy earnings became a particular target of political attack. (It should be noted that members at both ends of the political spectrum expressed concern about Mr. Hough's salary.)

President Clinton joined those who criticized the banks and Sallie Mae as being excessively profitable and attacked their efforts to lobby against the legislation. In a speech to an audience of high school students, President Clinton stated, "[Sallie Mae] is a group that helps us get college loans, it should not be a big 'profit-making' operation." He went on to criticize lenders saying, "Banks make more profits on student loans than on car loans or mortgages but there's no risk. They don't have to worry

125

if the student doesn't pay back the loan" ("Clinton Hits Sallie Mae on Profits, Lobbying" 1993).

Within months of taking office, President Clinton engineered enactment of a direct lending program through his first major budget and deficit reduction initiative.* At the Administration's urging, Congress passed the FY 94 budget resolution, which included provisions requiring the House and Senate Education Committees to enact programmatic changes to the GSL program that would reduce its costs by $4.3 billion over a five year period (FY 94-98). Given the size of the required savings target, the only way the committee could conceivably meet the budget resolution's instruction was by shifting a substantial portion of the GSL program to direct lending.

Further, by using the budget resolution as the instrument of change, the Administration ensured that these programmatic changes would be achieved through "budget reconciliation." Budget reconciliation is a process used by the Congress to reconcile government spending with the spending ceilings contained in the budget resolution for any given year. As part of this process, when Congress enacts the budget resolution, it directs committees to recommend changes to laws within their jurisdiction to conform to the spending totals contained in the governing budget resolution. Since the budget reconciliation process is tied to the budget resolution, it usually is completed in a short period. These changes are incorporated into a massive reconciliation bill, which requires enactment by both Houses of Congress and approval by the President.

The budget reconciliation process is a poor vehicle for undertaking major policy reform. Because the process takes place within a compressed time-frame and often is driven by budget concerns, policy decisions often take a back seat to these other considerations.

In addition to the compressed schedule, the sheer size and complexity of a budget reconciliation bill virtually guarantees that any major policy changes it contains will be made without significant debate. The little debate that occurs is generally confined to committees, thereby depriving the full Congress of an opportunity to thoroughly and publicly debate the issues. Committee recommendations get buried in huge bills that the majority party's leadership controls. The majority typically allows only limited and minor amendments to committee decisions. In the end,

---

*H. Con. Res. 64 called for $500 billion in deficit reduction. Therefore, reductions to the student loan program were only a small portion of the President's overall deficit reduction plans.

members of Congress get the opportunity only to vote up or down on the overall reconciliation legislation.

By using the budget reconciliation process, the Clinton Administration circumvented the traditional legislative process. While the legislative process is not always user-friendly, it does provide the intense scrutiny that major congressional policy initiatives ought to receive. The absence of this congressional scrutiny led the Clinton Administration and the Congress to make changes to the student loan program that only a year ago could not be enacted because of lack of support.

The FY 94 budget reconciliation process was the eighth time Congress had engaged in a budget reconciliation process since 1981. The GSL program had experienced the wrath of budget reconciliation in the past. The two biggest cost-saving provisions in the education budget were enacted through reconciliation processes in the 1980s: the elimination of high-default-rate schools from the program and the enactment of the 5% loan origination fee.

Because passage of the FY 94 budget reconciliation marked one of President Clinton's first major legislative initiatives with the 103rd Congress, the stakes were high and Democratic members were pressured to support their new President. Chairman William D. Ford (D-Mich.) of the Education and Labor Committee was among those committed to giving the President a victory. During the 1992 Higher Education Act debate, Chairman Ford had joined Congressman Andrews as a leading advocate in the attempt to replace the GSL program with direct lending. Now, in addition to helping the President, Chairman Ford viewed the President's initiative as another opportunity to push through legislation he could not get enacted in a previous Congress. As a consequence, Chairman Ford was an enthusiastic advocate of the Administration's direct loan proposal. Despite the uneasiness of several of the Democratic committee members, Chairman Ford achieved complete party loyalty and support throughout the budget reconciliation process. Chairman Ford managed to characterize support for direct lending as a metaphor for supporting President Clinton at a time when the Administration appeared to be floundering because of early policy missteps.

All but one of the Republicans on the Education and Labor Committee were opposed to a complete all-or-nothing shift to direct lending. They questioned the huge savings attributed to direct loans and believed that it was risky to proceed without the results of the pilot. House Republicans opposed to direct loans wanted very much to offer an alternative to the Clinton Administration's direct lending proposal. Attempts to put together a proposal that generated $4.3 billion in savings were unsuccessful. Unfortunately, the student loan industry, plagued by competing program interests, failed to rally behind a single alternative to direct lending that met the budget targets. Because of this failure, there was essentially no opportunity to find an alternative way of meeting the budget reconciliation instructions. There was simply not a painless way to find $4.3 billion in real savings in the program.

On 30 April 1993, the Administration sent Congress its legislative proposal to phase out the GSL program and replace it with a direct loan program. There was concern among both supporters and opponents of the President's proposal that it was too vague. The vagueness was not a lack of the Administration's commitment or intention to act on the proposal; rather, it was a function of the complexity of what was proposed. Phasing out the old program while at the same time developing a new program, balancing the desire for simplicity with the necessity for appropriate safeguards of federal funds, and the complexity of developing a workable income-contingent plan required a tremendous amount of consideration. These issues, which required the consultation and agreement of the Department of Education, the Department of Treasury, and the Office of Management and Budget, could not be fully explored and resolved in the short time frame that the reconciliation process afforded. Therefore, the Clinton Administration's proposals left many issues unresolved and granted broad discretion to the Secretary of Education to develop the program specifics. The Administration's plan was largely silent on one of the President's primary objectives, income-contingent direct lending. Although requested by House Republicans, there were no hearings on the legislation.

All of the House committee Democrats supported the Administration's proposal and passed it out of committee with only minor modifications just 12 days after it was received by Congress. It was voted out of committee on strictly party-line votes except for Congressman Tom Petri (R-Wis.), who voted for the legislation. Congressman Petri had advocated a direct loan program for more than a decade and viewed this process as an opportunity to see some of his ideas enacted into law. Congressman Petri ultimately voted against the budget reconciliation bill, however, because of his disagreement with the overall legislation.

Once reported from the committee, the direct loan legislation was folded into the massive Omnibus Budget Reconciliation Act of 1993. But the direct loan debate was not over. Congressman Bart Gordon (D-Tenn.) was committed to organizing bipartisan opposition to direct lending. The most dramatic manifestation of these efforts was a letter, signed by 239 members of Congress and sent to all of the conferees on the budget reconciliation conference, urging their rejection of the direct lending proposal. In my opinion, this letter played a significant role in the Administration's decision to make its final compromise.

Throughout the reconciliation process, the Senate Education Committee was far less agreeable to direct loans than the House. Nonetheless, like their House colleagues, Democratic Senators were under heavy pressure to support the President's initiative. The Senate version of reconciliation ended up being a patchwork of the views of its membership. For guaranteed loan proponents it retained 50% of the GSL program, and for direct loan proponents it moved 50% of the program to federal direct lending.

Senators Claiborne Pell (D-R.I.) and Nancy Kassebaum (R-Kans.) were concerned that in all of this reform the program should be made more attractive to students. Consequently, the Senate bill also included better loan terms for the students. As reported from the Senate committee, the proposal saved $6.2 billion: $4.3 billion to meet the budget reconciliation target and $1.9 billion to provide new benefits for students. This approach, while an acceptable political compromise, was troublesome from a programmatic standpoint in that it cut the GSL program so deeply that its continued viability was threatened.

Once the Omnibus Reconciliation bills were passed by each House, subconferences were set up to resolve the many differences between the two bills. The House-Senate subconference committee charged with resolving the direct loan issue comprised members of the House and Senate Education Committees. Because both bills called for direct lending in some form, the only real issue for the conferees was the level at which direct lending would be introduced into the student loan program. The resolution of this issue drove the resolution of all other issues.

The conference was characterized by sharp exchanges between the House and the Senate. The final compromise resolution was achieved after many hours of stalemate and posturing. The final compromise allowed for a gradual phase-in of direct lending: 5% of all new loan volume in FY 94, 40% in FY 95, 50% in FY 96, 50% in FY 97, and 60% in FY 98. This compromise was fashioned with little opportunity for discussion of the policy consequences of the choices made.

Conclusion

The enactment of direct lending highlights the shortcomings of the public policy process when the Congress must consider domestic policy legislation in times of limited resources and a soaring budget deficit. The final legislation was developed in a slipshod and haphazard manner; and while it met the necessary budget requirements, it really failed to reflect a vision for the future of the student loan program.

That vision is of enormous importance to American higher education. More than one-third of the funding for tuition and fees received by colleges and universities each year comes from federal student-aid programs. Student loans are by far the largest component of this aid. Whether the federal loan programs are guaranteed or provided through direct lending is of little consequence to students, who want only to make sure they have access to loans.

Over the next five years it will be the job of Congress, the executive branch, and the higher education policy community to make an honest assessment of the success of direct lending as compared to the GSL program. If direct lending lives up to the claims that it is a simpler, less expensive, and more efficient alternative to guaranteed lending, it should be the future of the student loan program. If it does not, however, it is this author's hope that Congress will have the courage to revisit education financing in the next reauthorization of the Higher Education Act and make an informed policy choice for the next century.

References

"Administration Seeking to Bypass Banks in Student Loan Program." *New York Times*, 7 January 1991, p. 1.

"Clinton Hits Sallie Mae on Profits, Lobbying." *Washington Post*, 12 May 1993, p. F1.

College Board. *Campus Views on the Implementation of Direct Lending: Results of a Survey*. Princeton, N.J., October 1993.

Congressional Research Service. *Federal Family Education Loans: Reduced Costs, Direct Lending, and National Income*. Report No. 93-247E. Washington, D.C., 1993.

General Accounting Office. *High Risk Series: Guaranteed Student Loans*. GAO/HR-93-2. Washington, D.C., December 1992.

Miles, Barbara, and Zimmerman, Dennis. *Guaranteed Student Loans vs. Direct Student Loans: Where Are the Savings?* Report No. 93-552E, U.S. Library of Congress, Congressional Research Service, 4 June 1993.

Penner, Rudolph. *Direct Government Loans vs. Guarantees for Student Loans: A Comparative Analysis*. Studies KMPG, Peat Marwick, May 1993.

U.S. Department of Education. *Federal Family Education Loan Program Loan Volume Update*. October 1993.

Direct Loans: A New Paradigm

By Thomas A. Butts

Thomas A. Butts is associate vice president for government relations at the University of Michigan. Since 1964, he has held a variety of positions at the university, including assistant director of admissions, director of student orientation, and director of financial aid. He also serves as an adjunct faculty member of the University of Michigan Center for the Study of Higher and Postsecondary Education.

From 1977 to 1981 while on leave from the university, Butts served as a policy advisor and the deputy assistant secretary for student assistance with the U.S. Department of Education. He is a past president of the University of Michigan Chapter of Phi Delta Kappa.

Why would many in the education community advocate replacement of a 28-year-old government guaranteed student loan entitlement program providing more than $19 billion per year in new education credit to students? How could this happen? And why would Congress start down such a risky path?

Federal education policy is often developed in response to an immediate real or perceived national crisis, rather than in response to a desire to provide the best quality education and opportunity for all citizens. However, good educational outcomes frequently are achieved as a result. Not surprisingly, though, the solution of the moment occasionally becomes an expensive, cumbersome headache in the long run, as the guaranteed student loan program has demonstrated.

The Omnibus Budget Reconciliation Act of 1993 (P.L. 103-66) created a context within which problems of both the federal deficit and student loan reform could be addressed. It is another example of education policy being developed within a larger framework of national policy. Whether the results will bring good or ill to students and taxpayers will be determined as the reforms are implemented by the Education Department.

First Federal Direct Student Loan Program, 1958

The first federal direct student loan program was created 35 years ago. The National Defense (subsequently called Direct and now Perkins) Student Loan Program was enacted in response to the Soviet Union's success in launching *Sputnik*. The country needed math and science teachers to beat the communists. A direct loan program, with cancellation features for those who performed national service through teaching, was thought to be a fine way to regain our national pride and save the nation. That program worked and continues to serve students well today.

The federal Perkins Loan Program was incorporated into the Higher Education Act of 1965 and has survived every reauthorization of that legislation. It operates as a direct loan program in both funding and delivery. Money is provided directly by the federal government to institutions that in turn deliver it directly to eligible students.

Currently, there are about $6 billion housed in Perkins revolving funds at postsecondary institutions. From that amount, about $750 million is loaned back to students each year, along with whatever new capital contributions might be appropriated by Congress from the discretionary side of the budget. New capital for this particular direct loan program comes from the same non-entitlement allocation that is available for other Education Department programs, such as Pell grants, Supplemental Grants, and Chapter 1, among others. However, the new Federal Direct Student Loan Program authorized in August 1993 is an entitlement program; and loan capital required to fund all eligible students will be available from the "mandatory" side of the federal budget.

Perhaps because the Perkins program has worked so well, the general public does not hear much about it. More than 3,500 institutions participate; and unlike the new Federal Direct Student Loan Program, institutions are responsible for collecting as well as originating loans. For institutions, the most complex aspect of the direct Perkins program has been in servicing and collection, a responsibility they will not have under the newly authorized Federal Direct Student Loan Program.

First Federal Guaranteed Student Loan Program, 1965

Twenty-eight years ago, as part of the war against poverty, Congress created another student loan program modeled after several existing state programs. Unlike Perkins loans, it was considered to be an entitlement program in the federal budget. Guaranteed student loans, now known as the Federal Family Educational Loan Program (FFELP), were intended to serve middle-income families. Any student whose family earned less than $15,000 per year could qualify for a federal interest subsidy — if a lender could be found to make the loan. Students with incomes below that level were presumed to have financial need for the subsidy. Those above could receive one if they demonstrated financial need according to a formal need analysis. At the University of Michigan, for example, students received Perkins, law enforcement, health professions (separate programs in medicine, dentistry, nursing, and pharmacy), and guaranteed loans. In addition, the university itself was a lender under the guarantee program for those students who could not find a lender in the banking community. Some students received loans, as they do today, from as many as three programs at the same time.

Education Department officials have indicated that President Johnson wanted to offer something to the middle class to make it easier to sell the poverty program. Lacking the time to think through a sound federal approach to student loans, the Johnson Administration turned to existing state guarantee programs for a model. They appeared to be inexpensive and were already operational in some states. This approach gave the Johnson Administration something for middle-income families and didn't offend those states that had programs in place. We learned later that what may have been a good model for the states did not necessarily constitute good national policy.

Purposes Change and Problems Accumulate

One fundamental difference existed between the Perkins and guaranteed programs: funding for Perkins came from the discretionary side of the budget, while FFELP was funded as an entitlement program. As appropriators searched for funding for the Pell grant program, authorized in 1972, it became easy to point to the guaranteed loans as a program that could ensure that every eligible student might receive a loan for what appeared to be little cost to the taxpayer. Scarce discretionary dollars could then be spent on grants. As I will discuss later, the true costs of the FFELP were hidden by the accounting practices of the day. It was not until 1990 that government accounting procedures were changed to more fairly compare the costs of direct and guaranteed loans.

Over the years, the two programs developed and, indeed, the government created more direct and guaranteed student loan programs, principally in the health professions. Some institutions have had responsibility for the administration of as many as seven or eight different federal loan programs on one campus at the same time.

While the Perkins program remained constant in its operation over the years, the guaranteed loan program was changed with great regularity to curtail abuses and to reduce taxpayer subsidies. The one loan guarantee program (FFELP) became three: student, supplemental, and parent. The family income for obtaining an in-school interest subsidy without a means test increased in the 1970s, was removed altogether in 1979, imposed again at $40,000 in 1982, and became subject to the same means test as the other Title IV student-aid programs shortly thereafter. When that occurred, the practice of targeting Perkins and subsidized guaranteed loans became identical.

While the financing of the Perkins programs became a problem for legislators, the delivery of guaranteed loans to students became a nightmare for students and institutions as well. At one point there were more than 10,000 lenders in the program, 46 guaranty agencies, and 35 secondary markets. Each had its own policies, procedures, and forms. Complexity and paper increasingly became barriers to student loan access; and notwithstanding improvements by some lenders and guarantee agencies, the problems of loan origination, delivery, and servicing remained.

Documented instances of fraud, error, and abuse in the guaranteed program are abundant. The operators of that program and others have pointed to for-profit schools as the source of the problem and poor management by the Education Department as the reason. However, General Accounting Office (GAO) and Inspector General (IG) reports, congressional hearings, and criminal convictions all reflect problems that can be traced to the structure of the program itself.

The most recent and complete documentation of problems in the guaranteed program is contained in the 1989 report of the Senate Permanent Committee on Investigations, chaired by Senator Sam Nunn (D-Ga.).[1] Senator Nunn's report documents the problems of poor gatekeeping and a serious decline in oversight of all student-aid programs, particularly guaranteed loans, by the Education Department in the 1980s. Senator Nunn's recommendations pointed to many structural problems associated with the complexity of the guarantee system. The report called for a study of the feasibility of "abolishing the guaranty agency concept" (p. 39).

The Nunn hearings and report reinforced for me that the structure of the program and behavior of the lenders, guarantee agencies, servicers, and secondary markets were the core of the problem. While it was fair to be critical of the department, it would have been a mistake not to recognize the failed structure of the guaranteed loan program itself as the source of trouble. That program would have been nearly impossible for the Education Department to administer under the best of circumstances.

Student Loan Alternatives

Alternative student loan programs have been discussed by a host of analysts, student-aid and loan officials, and members of Congress for years. The key themes of these discussions seem to be administrative simplification, financing, control of defaults and abuse, and income-contingent repayment plans.

The 1972 College Board publication, *New Patterns for College Lending*, discussed a variety of student loan options and developed ideas long under discussion. Many leading universities were acting as lenders under the federal portion of the FFELP. Searches were under way to find certain sources of private capital for student loans. The hope was that the origination problems of guaranteed loans could be addressed by institutional lending or by creative use of the Student Loan Marketing Association (Sallie Mae) that was authorized in 1972. Because of scandals in the proprietary sector and opposition by state guaranty agencies, school lending decreased. In the 1976 reauthorization, institutional lending was actively discouraged and the Education Department was required to establish a state agency in each state.

Attempts at income-contingent repayment plans were made by such schools as Yale. These programs failed when it was learned that one really needed a national source of loan capital for income-contingent repayment. The capacity of the federal government, particularly the Internal Revenue Service, also was needed to make the various income-contingent plans work. In recent years, advocates for guaranteed loans have tended to support "income-sensitive" or "graduated repayment" plans – anything short of a plan that would involve the IRS as the collection agent. The notion that an individual could have a percentage of income withheld has encountered stiff opposition from that community.

In an October 1993 paper, Robert Shireman, chief education advisor to Senator Paul Simon, provided a brief overview for supporting income-contingent repayment:

> *Career choice.* Student debt can skew the decisions that young people make about their education and their careers. This is why income-contingent repayment was made a part of the national service package: by allowing repayment of loans on the basis of

income, borrowers can perform a low-paying community service job without fear of defaulting on their student loans. This could be a chemist interested in teaching high school or a doctor who wants to practice at an inner-city health clinic. For some, service may be simply a one- or two-year diversion. For others, it may become a lifetime commitment. Either way, their debt should not make the decision for them.

Less discussed is the effect that traditional loans have on college enrollment by those students we need to help most. From the conversations that I have had with mostly minority youth at inner-city high schools, I have found that many of the most promising students are extremely debt-averse. They have learned, appropriately, that borrowing money can have disastrous consequences. But in the absence of much-needed increases in our grant programs, borrowing is the only route to college for many. Income-contingent repayment, if the formula is reasonable, helps to reduce (though not eliminate) the inherent risks to borrowing, allowing more to take the "risk" of a further education.

Humanitarian gesture. For some, a higher education does not yield financial rewards. In some cases it is because the school was not of good quality, a problem that is best addressed in the accreditation and licensing process. But in other cases things just do not work out for the student. For those who remain low-income, it does not make sense to demand unreasonable payments from them, prevent them from continuing their schooling, and ruin their credit records. Income-contingent repayment helps to ensure that their student loan is not one of the things that is preventing them from improving their lives.

Default reduction. Not all defaulters are poor, though. Most of those who are not poor are fit into four rough categories: lost, confused, clumsy, and yes, there are a few deadbeats. The "lost" usually went through a low-income period or moved around and never picked up their payments after defaulting. The "confused" were baffled by the guaranteed loan maze and gave up trying to figure out whom to pay. The "clumsy" just don't have good bill-paying or money-managing habits. And of course the "deadbeats" are ungrateful, greedy, and/or irresponsible.[2]

The Carter Administration took a serious look at the guaranteed loan program. It implemented the 1976 law and caused a guaranty agency to be established for each state. It did so, I believe, because it was the law, not because the Administration thought that was the best approach to student loans. It also took a number of actions to ensure that every student eligible for a loan was able to receive one.

Further, the Carter Administration seriously looked at proposing a direct loan program for the 1980 reauthorization. That plan ran into a budget obstacle. While all of the loan capital raised by the federal government through the incentives it pays to lenders for guaranteed loans is "off budget," capital raised for direct loans through the sale of government securities was "on budget." This came as a surprise to those new to government service, who naively thought there must be some logic to the federal budget process. This was especially true since Sallie Mae had been receiving all of its capital in this manner. Those were wonderful days for Sallie Mae. It obtained all of its loan capital from the U.S. Treasury at the treasury rate plus one-eighth percent. It then bought student loans from lenders and received the treasury rate plus 3.5% from the government. Of course, these loans also were insured 100% by the taxpayers against default losses. Sallie Mae recently repaid the $4.8 billion it obtained in this manner.

The Carter Administration proposed reforms for the guaranteed loan program that called for the consolidation of the eight federal student loan programs. It proposed that there be a means test for subsidized loans, that an unsubsidized program be available for students who did not demonstrate need, and that a parent loan program be established. It proposed other heresies of the time, such as variable student interest rates, which went nowhere. Of course, it did not help the Administration's cause that the proposals came to the Congress rather late in the process and that HEW Secretary Joseph Califano was fired the night before he was to testify and make the Administration's case.

However, direct loans were discussed in the Congress during that reauthorization. To their great credit, Senators Edward M. Kennedy (D-Mass.) and Henry Bellmon (R-Okla.) were able to get a direct loan proposal passed in the Senate; but it was lost in conference with the House. This plan contained some of the ideas of John Silber, president of Boston University, who has continued to support direct lending. William Byron, then-president of Catholic University in Washington, also has participated actively in the process through the years.

Ultimately, the 1980 reauthorization did not consolidate all of the federal programs as proposed by the Carter Administration, but it did add the supplemental and parent loan programs to the list of loan programs.

During the 1980s, the efforts of Congress and the Administration were devoted to reducing the cost of the guaranteed loan program, getting a handle on defaults, and ensuring that guaranteed loan capital would be available to students. The savings for the most part came from students in the form of origination fees. The program itself became the ultimate in micro-management. Congress had not accepted the fact that the guaranteed program could not be managed — even if the Administrations of the 1980s had been committed to good management. And even management by statute failed.

An interesting aspect of the 1986 reauthorization was an effort by some traditional institutions with excellent management records and low default rates to expand the authority of colleges and universities to be lenders themselves under the guaranteed loan program. This authority would have enabled approved institutions to use their own resources to make guaranteed loans. Expansion of the authority would have simplified the loan origination process for students and would have been profitable for the institutions. This proposal met stiff opposition from the guaranty community and ultimately was not granted, a fact not forgotten in 1992.

It was not until the 1992 reauthorization that it became possible for a serious student loan alternative to be considered. An education community frustrated with the delivery, accountability, and cost problems of the guaranteed loan program finally had an opportunity to work with Congress on fundamentally restructuring student loans.

The 1992 Reauthorization of the Higher Education Act

The chief obstacle to reform of the student loan programs over time turned out to be the budget numbers. A major industry had grown up around the guaranteed loan program. The guaranty agencies, lenders, servicers, and secondary markets who profited from the system had a wide network of allies in Congress and within some student financial-aid associations. While the direct loan political process has been rather visible to the wider education community, the budget numbers and process ultimately opened the door to serious reform.

Three important events external to the education committees of the Congress took place during the reauthorization period:

- the Nunn hearings and the collapse of a very larger guarantor, the Higher Education Assistance Foundations (HEAF), which convinced some that the program could not be fixed;
- the savings-and-loan bailout, which helped to undermine the credibility of the lending community and demonstrated that, if necessary, the Congress would borrow money "off budget" to solve what was thought to be a $500 billion problem;

- the Credit Reform provisions contained in the 1990 budget act, which required equal accounting treatment for government-guaranteed and direct loans.

While the first two helped to set the context for direct lending, it was Credit Reform that finally made it possible. The illusion that guaranteed loans were zero cost and direct loans were an outright expenditure ended with Credit Reform.

"Comparable Budget Costs for Cash and Credit," a 1989 Congressional Budget Office (CBO) report written by Marvin Phaup, said:

> The difference in the budgetary treatment between direct loans and guaranteed loans creates a bias in favor of guarantees because their costs are deferred. When the costs are known (after default) and finally recorded in the budget, they are well past the government's control. Consequently, loan guarantees have been growing much faster than direct loans in recent years. *The total cost to the government of the new guaranteed loans is now many times more than the cost of new direct loans.* (p. xii − emphasis added)

President Bush's FY 92 budget contained the following:

> Clearly, credit reform is not 'just' an accounting change. It is an opportunity to see each program with fresh eyes. Credit reform asks the right questions: Who is being helped? By how much? At what cost? It focuses attention and budgetary decisions on the costs underlying each loan, juxtaposed with the borrowers who benefit from these programs. It provides perspective for both policy analysis and program management. (Part Two, p. 226)

In view of this, it seemed contradictory for Office of Management and Budget (OMB) Director Richard Darman to be such a staunch opponent to direct lending − but more on that later.

The 1992 Reauthorization Process Gets Under Way

In early 1990, reauthorization discussions were under way among the higher education associations. Fundamental change in the loan guarantee program was not under serious consideration. The various association task forces were focused on modifications to the existing programs, not major reform. However, restructuring the student loan program became a high priority for University of Michigan President James J. Duderstadt, who chaired the Legislative Committee of the National Association of State Universities and Land Grant Colleges (NASULGC).

At the same time, I was talking with anyone who would listen about the possibility of a direct loan program. Senate Banking Committee staff were not too enthusiastic about finding another $10 billion to $15 billion of "off budget" borrowing. This was a bit difficult to understand given the size of the savings-and-loan bailout. However, staff counseled that if credit reform came to pass, it might be helpful to the direct loan idea. (Credit Reform finally did pass in November 1990, just in time for use in the reauthorization.) Thomas R. Wolanin, who served as Education and Labor Committee Chairman Bill Ford's staff director for the Subcommittee on Postsecondary Education, had a keen, long-standing interest in the idea and was a key player in the overall reauthorization process.

The White House Connection

While I was considering reauthorization options in winter of 1990 with Nan Nixon, Harvard University's representative in Washington, we discussed the need for student loan reform. She indicated that a colleague of hers from Harvard, economist Larry Lindsey, was now at the White House; and he had expressed an interest in direct loans. We then called on him, and he put us in contact with Charles Kolb, Deputy Assistant to the President for Domestic Policy. To our great pleasure, we discovered that the Education Department had developed a direct loan proposal that was under serious consideration as the centerpiece of the Bush reauthorization proposals.

Having previously consulted with our institutions at a meeting with Charles Kolb, we agreed to collaborate and began developing ideas to create public awareness of the direct loan concept. It also was agreed that we could talk with key Education Department career staff, such as Director of Postsecondary Analysis Division Bob Davidson, about the Administration's plan. Arrangements were made for Davidson to confer with us. He had done much of the work on the Administration's direct loan proposal and also had played a key role in helping to develop student loan reform ideas much earlier for the Carter Administration.

An interesting discussion of the role of the Bush Administration in direct lending is contained in Kolb's 1993 book, *White House Daze: The Unmaking of Domestic Policy in the Bush Years.*[3] Kolb points out that Former Education Secretary Lauro Cavazos:

> . . . liked and encouraged the concept. By the end of 1990, just
> two weeks before Bush and Sununu fired him, Cavazos informed

> OMB Director Darman that he would include direct loans as the centerpiece of his Higher Education Act reauthorization proposals.
>
> It may have just been a coincidence, but I find it suspicious that shortly after his discussion with OMB on direct loans Cavazos received his pink slip. (p. 148)

Direct loans would work only if it was clear that the program would be significantly less expensive than the guaranteed loan program. Improved service to students and simplification are powerful arguments in support of direct loans. By themselves, however, those arguments would not carry the day in Congress against proponents for the guaranteed loan system. Supporters of the existing system would contend, as they have in the past, that they could and would do better. Notwithstanding the unfulfilled promises of the past, the guaranty community would insist that the current system could be improved. That line of reasoning often is used to maintain the status quo for many government programs. It would prevail if the anticipated savings to the taxpayer of direct loans was unable to withstand careful scrutiny.

After meeting with the CBO director, the chief economist for the Senate Banking Committee, Education Department and OMB analysts, and analysts outside the government such as Arthur M. Hauptman, I was satisfied that direct loans would be less expensive than guaranteed loans and that the government estimators would prevail over attacks on the numbers that were sure to come from the lending interests.

Over the three years of the direct loan debate, the loan industry did indeed hire experts to attempt to discredit the collective judgment of the analysts from OMB, CBO, the Education Department, and the GAO that direct loans save substantial money. While the estimates changed a bit, based on changed program assumptions and the inclusion of administrative costs, the effort to discredit the numbers created uncertainty but ultimately failed. People who were not expert in the federal budget process came to understand that the only numbers that count are those provided by CBO and OMB.

The Education Department had done extensive work on cost estimates and, while the source could not be revealed at the time, department officials were confident that $1.4 billion in savings per year could be achieved by replacing the guaranteed loan program with direct loans. After concluding consultations, savings of more than $1 billion per year seemed to be a cautious number for me to use in describing probable direct loan savings. The savings were seen as a possible source of funding for student aid by some and a source of federal deficit reduction by others.

In the fall of 1990, as a result of the meetings with Charles Kolb, Bob Davidson was able to brief certain congressional staff who might be interested in the idea. These briefings, held over coffee at the University of Michigan Washington Office, provided Capitol Hill staff with the substance of the Administration's plan and a sense of the extensive work that had gone into developing it. Staff from both sides of the aisle were interested in direct loans and felt that something major needed to be done to reform the loan programs. There seemed to be consensus that if the Administration proposed such a plan, it might have a good chance for enactment. With the loss of Cavazos and a key Republican staff member, however, it became clear that the task would be difficult.

Behind the scenes, discussions about the idea continued until 7 January 1991, when a front page *New York Times* story by Robert Pear revealed the Administration's plan for direct lending.[4] I was interviewed for the story by phone on New Year's Eve at my home in Ann Arbor, and I was supportive of the Administration's plan. Public debate and advocacy on direct loans thus began. Kolb goes into considerable detail about this initial period in his book.

The Role Of NASULGC

NASULGC was the key association player in helping to move the direct loan initiative forward. In 1990 the NASULGC Student Aid Committee recommended to the association that student loan reform be a high priority for reauthorization. I gave a presentation on direct loans and credit reform to the Student Aid Committee and the Legislative Committees at the November 1990 annual meeting of the association.

This led to further discussions, and in January 1991 a discussion paper I drafted was circulated to a few interested parties for comment. It had become clear to some association members that credit reform had opened an opportunity that would be utilized at some point. There was agreement that if a new direct loan program was to be developed, it would be wise for NASULGC and others from the college and university community to design the program in such a way that it worked well for both students and institutions.

In March 1991 President Duderstadt chaired a meeting of the NASULGC Legislative and Student Aid Committees, where a revised draft was discussed. It was agreed at that meeting to hold a weekend gathering on direct loans in April at Colorado State University. Those participating included a small group of financial-aid administrators from NASULGC member schools and several independent institutions, along with a business-officer representative and association staff from the American Council on Education and NASULGC. It is fair to say that this meeting marked a turning point in developing broad institutional support for direct loans. Not all of the participants went away convinced that direct lending was the right policy course, but consensus developed that direct loans designed along the lines the group had discussed could work.

Key criteria were:

- assurance that direct loans would be an entitlement program scored in the budget in such a way as to not take funding from the grant programs;
- simplicity of delivery and integration with the student application process used for Pell grants and campus-based student aid;
- alternate loan origination provided by the government or consortia options for those institutions that did not choose to have origination responsibility;
- cash drawdown of federal funds like that used for the other Title IV programs; and
- loan servicing that was clearly a government responsibility.

The proposal was approved by the NASULGC Executive Committee with the active support of then-association president Robert Clodius. The charge, to what had become the Direct Loan Working Group, was to take the idea as far as possible or, as Don Zacharias, president of Mississippi State University and chair of the Student Aid Committee, put it, until a "snake in the grass" was found that could prove that direct lending would not work.

The plan continued to be refined, and testimony was given before the Senate Committee on Labor and Human Resources in the spring. This was followed on 12 June 1991 by testimony before the Subcommittee on Postsecondary Education, where a rather complete proposal was put forth.[5] Indeed, the General Accounting Office prepared a report that compared the delivery of the guaranteed loan program with the NASULGC direct loan plan.[6]

C. Peter Magrath, who became the president of NASULGC in January 1992, made direct lending one of his highest priority legislative objectives. Under his leadership, consensus for direct lending within the member institutions grew. He made significant contributions to building a base of higher education support when he appeared on such programs as the 12 May 1993 "MacNeil/Lehrer News Hour" segment on direct lending.

143

Other Higher Education Associations

Serious discussion about direct loans took place in the spring of 1991 among the six major associations: The American Council on Education (ACE), NASULGC, the American Association of State Colleges and Universities (AASCU), the National Association of Independent Colleges and Universities (NAICU), the American Association of Community Colleges (AACC), and the Association of American Universities (AAU).

Support for direct lending among the associations at that time was mixed; but there was final agreement to include direct lending in the association package of reauthorization proposals, with the stipulation that institutions be provided the flexibility to choose direct lending or remain with the existing loan guarantee program.

The recommendations were sent to the Congress in April 1991. Twelve institutional higher education associations agreed to a comprehensive package of proposals that included direct lending. It was interesting that the National Association of College and University Business Officers (NACUBO) was on the list, but the National Association of Student Financial Aid Administrators (NASFAA) was not.

The role of the United States Student Association in helping to move the direct loan proposal forward should not be understated. Its leadership took the time to understand the issues and supported the idea on its merits. They carefully reviewed the arguments presented to them by the supporters of the guaranteed loan program and consistently concluded that direct lending would better serve students. Indeed, the first public debate in which I engaged took place at a symposium on student aid sponsored by students at the University of Colorado at Boulder in April 1991. The chair of the Consumer Bankers Association legislative committee spoke on behalf of the guaranteed loan program. Interestingly, David Longanecker, now Assistant Secretary for Postsecondary Education, also participated in that meeting.

Institutional support for direct lending was a dynamic process, and much education took place between 1990 and 1993. While NASULGC continued to call for a full phase-in of direct lending, other associations initially testified in favor of a dual program. The discussion among members of the education and association community became a debate over the size of the program. Some institutions that supported direct lending early from a policy perspective were forced by pressure from the guaranteed lending community to withdraw their support or stand silently on the sidelines, while others made the case for the new program.

As support for direct lending developed within the education community, it became clear that many of the advocates of the guaranty system failed to comprehend the implications of credit reform for their industry. Once the opponents understood fully that direct lending was a serious threat to the status quo, the industry spared no expense to defeat the proposal. Space does not permit a full description of the lobbying activities that took place, but they were substantial and will provide an extensive case study for a disinterested observer to explore and recount.

One of the curious aspects of the direct loan discussion was the role played by NASFAA. Historically that organization has taken the lead in informing its members about developments in the field of financial aid. With respect to direct loans, however, it did not develop a position or provide significant information to its membership until after a full direct loan program had been incorporated in the bill reported from the House Subcommittee on Postsecondary Education in October 1991. This occurred at a time when its members received substantial and sustained information against the program from the guaranteed lending community. This resulted in a great deal of confusion about direct lending among financial-aid administrators. While some thoughtful people within the student-aid community opposed changing programs, much opposition seemed to result from the incomplete information available to financial-aid administrators.

Arguments For and Against Direct Lending

The arguments for and against direct lending have remained essentially the same throughout the three-year history of the legislative process. In an article published in February 1992, NACUBO Business Officer Elizabeth M. Hicks of Harvard and I discussed some of the myths about direct lending as we saw them.[7] Throughout, Hicks played a significant role in the direct loan debate. The same basic arguments against direct lending were used by the Bush OMB and the supporters of the guaranteed loan program. The arguments against direct lending, as we saw them, and our rebuttals were as follows:

Direct Loans Increase the Federal Debt.

Loan guarantees have the same effect on the economy as federal direct loans. Stafford Loan guarantees are listed in the President's FY 92 budget as a 100% contingent liability of the federal government; responsibility for federal direct loans would be the same. Loan guarantees affect treasury bill rates virtually as much as direct borrowing, and loan guarantee programs are more costly overall. While raising capital for the $10 billion student loan programs wholesale through the sale of government securities to private markets adds to the $4 trillion national debt, the lower cost of direct lending could reduce the deficit if the savings were not passed on to students. Loan guarantees are a part of the national debt, but are not counted as such. Further, direct student loans are an asset of the government – an investment in educated manpower that will be repaid.

Direct Loans Shift All Risk to the Federal Government.

The guaranteed loan program is structured to pass on the majority of risk to the federal government. States are not required to appropriate money for defaults, and the cost of risk borne by the guaranty agencies is covered by student insurance premiums. The only risk not assumed by the federal government is the risk to lenders when they do not perform due diligence properly. To argue that there is less risk to the government in the current program because lenders make errors is to make the case that the program is poorly designed. The complexity of the program leaves many errors undetected. In contrast, direct loans reduce federal risk by providing clear, simple lines of accountability, government servicing contracts with positive performance bonuses, and direct government oversight.

Direct Loans Would Increase Administrative Burden on Institutions.

If a college, university, or trade school can process a Pell grant or Stafford loan, it can handle federal direct loans. For the student as well as the institution, the application process would work much like a combination of the Pell grant and Perkins loan programs. Students would sign promissory notes that the institution would forward to its servicing agent. The opportunity for error would be considerably less than with the complicated Stafford loan program, and the simplicity of the operation would reduce overall institutional costs. Analyses conducted by institutional representatives indicate that the overall burden for administering federal direct loans is less than for the guaranteed loan system.

Direct Loans Would Increase Institutional Liability.

Institutions currently are liable for mistakes they make in performing their duties for all the student-aid programs, including the Stafford loan program. Because of the relative simplicity of the direct loan program, it would reduce institutional liability. Fewer chances for error would be present, and institutions would be better positioned to integrate management of direct loans with other Title IV programs.

Direct Loans Would Lead to Fraud and Abuse by Institutions.
Fraud and abuse in the existing loan system are not confined to a few organizations. Without 45 guaranty agencies, 10,000 lenders, and 35 secondary markets to oversee, the department's efforts could be focused on contractors and institutions. Clear lines of accountability and financing managed by the Treasury Department in conjunction with integrity provisions, such as those in H.R. 3553, would reduce fraud and abuse in all student-aid programs.

Direct Loans Would Give Trade Schools an Excuse to Raise Tuition.
The administration has proposed increasing loan limits for the Stafford loan program. If there is an incentive to increase tuition artificially, it would be the same with either program.

Phasing Out the Loan Guarantee System Would be Difficult.
Lenders would want their claims paid on outstanding loans and, therefore, would perform due diligence in loan collection as required by law. With about $50 billion in outstanding loans to be serviced and with a recent Department of Education study showing Stafford loans to be more profitable than home mortgages and car loans, lenders would have economic incentives to remain in the program through the phase-in period. Guaranty agencies probably would receive an administrative allowance based on outstanding loan volume to assist in the drawdown process. As the failure of a major guaranty agency in 1990 demonstrated, loan guarantees can be transferred. H.R. 3553 has provisions to accommodate failed or weak agencies.

Ultimately, private lenders participate in the Stafford loan program because it is profitable. In the transition from Stafford loans to federal direct loans, one must assume the same economic process would continue. In addition, higher education does a far greater volume of other business with the lending industry than it does under the Stafford loan program. During a transition, the banking community probably would be cooperative.

The Education Department Cannot Run the Program.
With a 1 July 1994 starting date for direct lending and a three-year phase-in plan, a smooth transition is possible. Federal direct loans are not guaranteed loans, and a comparison to guaranteed or other insured loan programs is inappropriate. Federal direct loans more closely resemble Perkins loans. The secretary probably will make use of the best features of the Pell grant and Perkins delivery systems for direct lending. The Department of Education has made significant progress with inno-

vations to the Pell grant program, including electronic processing and Stage Zero, which allows a student to use a computer to complete an application with immediate edits for errors. Electronic institutional applications for Perkins loans and the recent electronic re-application will save the department millions of dollars in printing, contract costs, and computing while improving services to students.

Congressional Action Leading to Passage of the 1992 Act

My assignment has been to discuss the why and how of direct lending from the view of an institutional person supportive of the initiative. The effort here is to highlight a few key actions, not to provide a comprehensive chronicle of every action taken.

One of the difficult issues to be resolved was the question of the savings associated with direct loans. While some knew what the numbers were, they had not been released by the Education Department. The Bush Administration essentially was opposed to direct lending after the departure of Secretary Cavazos. However, it had the numbers and the extensive documentation necessary to demonstrate that direct loans saved money. Chairman Ford wrote Secretary Lamar Alexander and asked for the information. On 28 June 1991, Secretary Alexander finally answered Ford's two-month-old request. While the narrative portion of the letter did not mention the $1.4 billion in savings, the documentation depicted the dramatic possibilities for savings.[8] The numbers were now public.

The Andrews Bill

At the 12 June 1991 House hearing on direct loans, it became clear that Congressman Robert Andrews (D-N.J.) was interested in the issue and had an easy grasp of the subject matter. Later, when talking with Chairman Ford's staff director Tom Wolanin about possible sponsors for direct loan legislation, Rep. Andrews became the obvious choice. He had the support of Ford on this issue and understood the substantive and political challenges ahead. Les Keoplin, federal relations officer from Rutgers University, and I paid a call on Congressman Andrews, who was pleased to learn of Rutgers' support for direct lending.

In the months that followed, we worked with Congressman Andrews and his able legislative director, Ken Holdsman, to advise them on the legislation as it was developed. H.R. 3211 was introduced on 2 August 1991 by Congressman Andrews, who provided leadership and substance to the issue. That legislation, with minor modification, was designed along the lines of the NASULGC model and was incorporated by Chairman Ford into the postsecondary subcommittee's draft bill.

The proposed legislation in the subcommittee bill provided for the replacement of the guaranteed loan program with direct lending over a five-year period. The first loans were to be made to students attending 500 institutions in 1994-95. All of the savings achieved by direct lending were to be passed on to students in the form of higher loan limits and the elimination of all origination fees. The loan limits were the combined limits of Perkins and guaranteed loans. That would have made it possible for the legislation to convert the $6 billion institutional Perkins revolving funds into funds on campuses, functioning as endowments, the income from which could be used for student grants. The legislation further authorized the use of income-contingent repayment by student borrowers as an elective option.

Direct lending as a replacement for the guaranteed loan program was reported intact from subcommittee in early October. Then on 23 October 1991, it was reported from the full Education and Labor Committee. Direct lending was on its way to becoming law with all of the savings achieved by eliminating guaranty agencies, lenders, and secondary markets from the program going to students.

In both committee markups of the legislation, expected debate with Congressman Andrews by the opponents of direct lending never took place. One suspects that the opposition would have had a tough time making its case against Congressman Andrews. However, using the threat of a presidential veto, the opponents, led by Representatives William Goodling (R-Pa.) and Tom Coleman (R-Mo.) and supported by Education Secretary Lamar Alexander and OMB Director Richard Darman, were successful in getting the direct loan initiative scaled back to a demonstration program before the legislation finally went to the House floor for a vote in March 1992.

Important to the support of direct lending was the role played by Congressman Tom Petri (R-Wis.), who for years has taken the high road in advocating a direct loan program with income-contingent repayment as its centerpiece. He and his aide, Joe Flader, worked diligently and effectively to explain the benefits of direct lending, income-contingent repayment, and the need to restructure the system. Indeed, Congressman Petri's IDEA plan was introduced in the Senate by Senator David Durenberger (R-Minn.) and became the vehicle for a major collaborative effort with Senator Paul Simon (D-Ill.).

Senator Simon had become concerned that the Senate reauthorization appeared to be turning into little more than an updating of the existing student-aid programs. He concluded that a major restructuring of the loan programs was needed, along with increased funding for Pell grants. Senator Simon's chief education advisor, Bob Shireman, had been following the direct loan developments carefully and was one of the most knowledgeable Hill staff members on the subject. Indeed, a very helpful flow chart describing direct loans, which he devised, was attached with attribution to the NASULGC testimony in the House on 12 June 1991.[9] Also, Orlo Austin, director of financial aid at the University of Illinois-Urbana and a member of the NASULGC Direct Loan Working Group, was serving an internship with Simon at the time.

One of the chief differences between the Andrews' version of direct lending and the Simon/Durenberger approach was the way in which the direct loan savings were used. The House would have used the savings internally to improve loan program benefits, while Simon/Durenberger proposed to use them to create a Pell grant entitlement program on the mandatory side of the budget. This entitlement was to have been an add-on to the regular appropriation for Pell grants and met the pay-as-you-go requirements of the budget act.

The Senate passed its version of the Higher Education Act reauthorization on 20 February 1992, without direct loans or a Pell entitlement. While the Senate reauthorization bill did not finally include a direct loan proposal, a direct loan plan by Senators Simon, Durenberger, Kennedy, and Bradley was included in a Finance Committee urban aid bill that passed the Senate. The direct loan provision, which emphasized income-contingent repayment, was later dropped in conference with the House Ways and Means Committee.

The conference on the reauthorization was concluded in June 1992, and the House direct loan demonstration program was agreed to after veto threats by the Administration had been resolved.

The conference report was adopted by Congress, and President Bush signed the legislation on 23 July 1992 at a campus of Northern Virginia Community College. Charles Kolb kindly invited Nan Nixon and me to the signing. I recall attending a similar ceremony in 1980 at a different campus of that institution, just before Jimmy Carter was defeated in his bid for re-election. Later, I placed a call to Larry Oxendine at the Education Department, and the phone was answered with "Federal Direct Student Loan Program."

The Clinton Administration

Charles Kolb points out in his book that "Bush was never engaged in any serious way when it came to higher education. . . ." One cannot make that statement about Bill Clinton. Clinton campaigned on the idea that students should be able to participate in national service to help repay their student loans; he also supported the universal availability of income-contingent repayment. These were simple concepts that resonated well with the American public and to which the new President was deeply committed. Furthermore, it also is clear that his leadership team shares his views in this area.

Campaign officials discussed the National Service Trust Fund concept with members of the education community. It did not take long to explain that the trust approach to a national revolving fund of student loan capital had been replaced by credit reform and direct lending. Bob Shireman reports that Senator Simon met in his office with candidate Clinton in the fall of 1991 and discussed direct loans and income-contingent repayment with him.

During the transition and early in the Clinton Administration, the advocates for the direct financing of student loans and the loan guaranty system made their case to the new Administration. Direct lending ultimately was adopted by the President and his leadership team at the Education Department, the White House Domestic Policy staff, and OMB as the means to create the loan infrastructure to support income-contingent repayment.

While the new Administration still was developing its national service and student loan proposals, the National Commission of Responsibilities for Financing Postsecondary Education issued its final report in February 1993. The report, *Making College Affordable Again*, received a great deal of positive national attention. The commission's unanimous recommendations called for a new approach to student-aid policy for grants, work, and loans. It had recommendations for national service as well as tax policy. One of its major recommendations called for direct lending. The commission was authorized by Congress under the leadership of Senator James Jeffords (R-Vt.). It did not have recommendations for or participate in the 1992 reauthorization. Instead, it took a longer view; and its report appeared at the same time the Clinton Administration was considering major reform.

The commission, on which I served, was chaired by former-Senator Paula Hawkins (R-Fla.); and its executive director throughout most of its two-year life was Jamie Merisotis. It was composed of five Republicans and four Democrats appointed by the House, the Senate, and the Administration.

With a single source of loan capital, the loan-cancellation features of national service and the income-contingent repayment through the

151

Internal Revenue Service would dovetail nicely. At the same time, the Administration was looking at ways to reduce the deficit. The savings from expanding the direct loan demonstration program were considerable — more than $2 billion per year after full implementation. OMB Director Leon Panetta had included the savings from direct loans in all of the budget alternatives he had offered the previous year as chair of the House Budget Committee.

The President's FY 94 budget proposal assumed savings from a complete phase-in of direct lending. This was incorporated in the budget reconciliation bills of both the House and Senate. The result was that the education committees had to find $4.3 billion in savings over five years, which was assumed to come from replacing the guaranteed loan program with direct lending. As indicated earlier, numbers drive the process; and the education committees had no choice but to make major changes in the student loan programs.

The Administration proposed to the education committees that the savings be achieved by moving to 100% direct lending in five years. The House adopted that position under the leadership of Chairman Bill Ford.

The process was not that straightforward in the Senate. Advocates for the existing program admitted that they had been making excessive profits from the program and floated various proposals that would achieve the $4.3 billion from the existing program. The structure of the proposals put forward by the loan industry were revealing; their prior threats to withdraw if cuts to their margins were made somehow evaporated. History will show that any reductions in subsidies had been greeted by the industry with an attitude of "the sky is falling." Direct lending had at least produced some leverage for Congress to deal with the lending community.

Some of the industry plans for achieving the $4.3 billion in required cuts would have done so by reducing in-school benefits, an idea that was not well received in Congress. Since the House bill calling for 100% direct lending had included some increased benefits to students, the Senate felt it should do better. The cost associated with these program benefits had to be paid for over and above the $4.3 billion required for deficit reduction as part of budget reconciliation.

The final Senate package included a mix of direct lending and cuts in the guaranteed program that reduced subsidies for the guaranty agencies, secondary markets, and lenders. Senator Kennedy supported the Administration's phase-in of full direct lending. However, the process

152

was complicated by Senator Nancy Kassebaum's opposition, Senator James Jeffords' support for something less than a full replacement of the guarantee system, and deep concerns held by Senator Claiborne Pell. Things were further complicated by the fact that the national service legislation also was on the Senate floor during the direct loan conference, and it needed Republican votes.

After a difficult House/Senate conference on the reconciliation bill, a combination of direct lending and major cuts in the guaranteed loan program were agreed to. The legislation required direct lending to constitute 5% of the total loan volume in 1994-95, 40% in 1995-96, 50% in 1996-97 and 1997-98, and 60% in 1998-99. A major point of contention in the conference centered on whether the percentages should be caps or floors. It finally was agreed that beginning in 1996-97, any institution that wanted to participate in the new program could do so; thus 100% direct lending became possible, but not required.

From inauguration to enactment, five of the six key higher education associations supported the new Administration's plan for direct lending. The AAU choose not to take a position but participated in the discussions. The Career College Association supported the Administration as well. The Administration was open and flexible in responding to suggestions and concerns.

Needless to say, the lobbying continued to be intensive. The education associations were better prepared to inform their members about how the direct loan program would work. Terry Hartle, who had just joined ACE from the staff of Senator Kennedy, organized briefings on student loan reform that were held around the country. Staff from NASULGC, AASCU, and NAICU, along with the Direct Loan Working Group, continued to provide information.

Several presentations by Elizabeth Hicks, including testimony before the Advisory Committee on Student Financial Aid, were informative.[10] Kay Jacks from Colorado State University and Jerry Sullivan from the University of Colorado-Boulder wrote a piece titled, "Let's Take Back Student Aid: Direct Lending Issues and Myths," which was printed and distributed by AASCU and NASULGC to association members.[11]

There were two letters of support that, in particular, deserve comment. The first, to Senators Kennedy and Kassebaum on 21 May 1993, was signed by six past presidents of NASFAA: Joe L. McCormick, Neil Bolyard, Kay Jacks, Gene Miller, Ken Wooten, and Eunice Edwards.[12] It was not easy for these colleagues to take a position different from that of the association board to which they had been so close.

A second letter strongly supporting the Clinton proposal for full direct lending was dated 25 May 1993 and was signed by eight senior appointees of the former Bush Administration.[13] This effort was coordinated by Charles Kolb, former Deputy Assistant to the President for Domestic Policy, and was sent to the chairs of the House and Senate education committees. In addition to Kolb, the letter was signed by Rich Bond, former chairman of the Republican National Committee; Diana Culp Bork, former Deputy General Counsel at the Education Department; James P. Pinkerton, former Deputy Assistant to the President for Policy Planning; Carolynn Reid-Wallace, former Assistant Secretary for Postsecondary Education; Nancy Mohr Kennedy, former Assistant Secretary for Legislation and Congressional Affairs at the Education Department; Michael J. Horowitz, former general counsel at OMB; and George A. Pieler, former Acting Deputy Under-Secretary for Planning, Budget, and Evaluation at the Education Department.

A Closing Note

The Omnibus Reconciliation Bill of 1993 was signed by the President in August 1993. The Education Department, building on the work done to implement the direct loan demonstration program, proceeded with enthusiasm to get the program off the ground. Applications for the 1994-95 school year were made available to institutions on 10 September 1993, with a 1 October 1993 deadline.

What occurred exceeded everyone's expectations. More than 1,100 institutions applied, more than 900 met the eligibility requirements, and 105 have been selected.[14] The eligible applicants represented about 20% of the national loan volume when only 5% was needed for the first year. The department is moving swiftly and effectively to make direct loans work. It is clear to this observer that under the leadership of Secretary Richard Riley, Deputy Secretary Madeleine Kunin, and Assistant Secretary David Longanecker — together with a rejuvenated career staff at the Education Department — the Federal Direct Student Loan Program will be a success.

Footnotes

1. "Allegations of Bank Fraud in the Federal Guaranteed Student Loan Program," Report of the Senate Permanent Subcommittee on Investigations, chaired by Senator Sam Nunn, 1989.
2. Robert Shireman, "Income-Contingent, Direct Student Loans in the United States: Recent History, and Issues for Implementation," Advisory paper, October 1993.

3. Charles Kolb, *White House Daze: The Unmaking of Domestic Policy in the Bush Years* (New York: Free Press, 1993).
4. Robert Pear, *New York Times*, 7 January 1991, p. 1.
5. Thomas A. Butts, "Regarding Direct Loans for Students," Presentation to the House Subcommittee on Postsecondary Education, Education and Labor Committee; statement on behalf of the National Association of State Universities and Land Grant Colleges, 12 June 1991.
6. "Student Loans Could Save Money and Simplify Program Administration," General Accounting Office Report, GAO/HRD-91-144BR, 27 September 1991.
7. Thomas A. Butts and Elizabeth M. Hicks, "The Direct Lending Debate: Making the Case for and Dispelling Myths About Direct Lending," *National Association of College and University Business Officer* (February 1992).
8. Lamar Alexander, Letter to Congressman William D. Ford, 28 June 1991.
9. Higher Education Act Reauthorization, Conference Report S. 1150, 1992.
10. Elizabeth Hicks, "Statement on Direct Lending," Presentation to the Advisory Committee on Student Financial Assistance, 4 May 1992; Elizabeth Hicks, "Understanding Direct Lending," Presentation to the Advisory Committee on Student Financial Assistance, Symposium on Loan Simplification, 5 April 1993.
11. G. Kay Jacks and Jerry Sullivan, "Let's Take Back Student Aid: Direct Lending Issues and Myths" (Washington, D.C.: American Association of State Colleges and Universities and National Association of State Universities and Land Grant Colleges, 1993).
12. Letter to Senators Kennedy and Kassebaum, 21 May 1993.
13. Charles Kolb et al., Letter to Senators Kennedy and Kassebaum and Representatives Ford and Goodling, 25 May 1993.
14. "105 Schools Selected to Participate in Direct Lending Program," U.S. Department of Education news release, 15 November 1993.

Enactment of the Federal Direct Student Loan Program as a Reflection of the Education Policymaking Process

By John E. Dean

John E. Dean is a founding partner of the Washington, D.C., law firm of Clohan & Dean. Prior to establishing the firm in 1985, he served as associate counsel to the Republican staff of the House Committee on Education and Labor, focusing on higher education legislation. John Dean was educated at Georgetown University and Georgetown University Law Center. He is a native of Washington, D.C.

The enactment of the Student Loan Reform Act in August 1993 is described by some as the single greatest change in federal student-aid policy since 1965. Others describe it as a mistake that ultimately will both reduce the reliability of the student loan and expose the federal government to higher costs. The legislation creates a new Federal Direct Student Loan Program as a replacement for the Federal Family Education Loan Program (FFELP), also formerly known as Guaranteed Student Loans.[1]

In this paper I examine the federal policymaking process that led to the enactment of the direct student loan program and comment on whether some of the advantages claimed for direct loans, including a reduction in federal costs, simplicity of administration by schools, and lower costs to borrowers, are likely to be achieved. My perspective is that of the student loan industry. From 1991 to 1993, the law firm of Clohan & Dean served as special counsel to the Consumer Bankers Association, a trade association representing lenders participating in the FFELP. I am drawn to the conclusion that the direct loan program will not achieve the benefits claimed for it and that the legislative process produced a program that could undermine the stability of federal student assistance in coming years.

Guaranteed Versus Direct Loans: A Difference for Whom?

The debate on the merits of replacing the FFEL program with direct loans requires a basic understanding of the structures of the two programs. Although the FFEL program has been criticized for being excessively complex, in its simplest form it is a program of loan guarantees and subsidies paid by the government on behalf of student borrowers — a complete subsidy during periods the borrower is in school or in a specified period of deferment and a subsidy during times of higher interest rates. (See sections 427A, 428, and 438 of the Higher Education Act.) Both subsidies encourage private-sector lenders to make capital available to borrowers who would otherwise be unable to secure funds for college, and both subsidies worked well. For example, since its inception in 1964, FFEL has provided more than $127 billion in loans through FY 93, including $18 billion in FY 92 alone.

The loan guarantees in student loans originally were provided directly by the federal government under a program called the Federally-Insured Student Loan (FISL) program. Poor service to institutions, students, and lenders and a desire to decentralize the program led to the eventual transition to a guaranty agency-based system supported by a program of federal reinsurance.[2] Under the guaranty agency-based program, non-profit and state agencies provide guarantees — funded by a small administrative allowance paid by the department, retention of a percent of collections on defaulted loans, and an insurance premium paid by the borrower. The federal government reimburses guaranty agencies on claims paid to lenders and holders. The reinsurance provisions are structured to provide incentives to guarantors to implement close oversight of lender collection efforts.

The direct loan program, as enacted, replaces both lenders and guaranty agencies by substituting federal treasury funds for private capital.[3] By so doing, no federally supported insurance or payment of subsidies to secure private capital is necessary. Under direct loans, funds will be secured through the Treasury Department (through the issuance of treasury bonds or the use of tax receipts) and distributed to participating educational institutions for redistribution to students.

The educational institution, as agent to the federal government, undertakes most administrative functions entailed in the origination process performed in the FFEL program by lenders or loan servicers. Certain institutions may be required to use an alternative origination servicer, and all institutions in the program will have the option of using the alternative originator. Loan servicing will be performed by contractors working for the Department of Education. School responsibilities following disbursement of loans are limited to processing adjustments in the loan amount if the borrower's enrollment status changes, notifying the federal servicing contractor of such changes, and maintaining records of receipt of funds from the government and their disbursement to borrowers.

Advocates of direct loans argued that school administrative costs would be significantly reduced by eliminating the need to deal with multiple lender and guaranty agency program participants.[4] Proponents of the FFEL program pointed out that schools would be assuming significant new administrative responsibilities associated with loan disbursement and new potential liabilities without adequate compensation from the federal government.[5] FFEL proponents also argued that shifting costs from the federal government to the institutions was the means by which a significant portion of direct loan savings were achieved. They noted that under the congressional budget procedures, administrative costs shifted to schools did not appear as a cost of the new program, thus creating a misleading estimate of the savings associated with it.

Prelude to Change: Student Loan Boom Years

Steadily rising college costs throughout the mid- to late-1980s and a willingness on the part of Congress to help families meet these costs through federally subsidized loans created a boom period for the student loan industry that lasted approximately 10 years.[6] Loan volume increased by 84% (in dollar amounts) from 1980 through 1985, with average loan size increasing proportionately. From FY 80 to FY 89, loan volume rose from $4.8 billion to $12.4 billion. Average loan size between FY 80 and FY 90 grew from $2,091 to $2,734.[7] Simultaneous with this growth, loan servicing costs continued to decrease, making student loans a growth area for many financial institutions. The attractiveness of the program is evidenced by the number of financial institutions participating in the program. Participation peaked at 11,298 in fiscal year 1985.[8]

In addition to loan volume generated by traditional four-year public and private institutions, growth in the student loan market took place as a result of an explosion in the volume of loans to students attending proprietary trade schools. For example, the percent of federal Stafford Loans going to students at proprietary institutions rose from 14.3% in FY 83 to 34.9% in FY 87. By FY 88, 61.5% of all student loans were made to proprietary school students.[9]

Easily the most rapidly growing segment of student loan business during the mid-1980s, proprietary school loans were universally available to any financial institution desiring to build or acquire a student loan portfolio in a short period of time. In some instances, this rapid growth included program abuse. Two major instances of abuse, as described by Senator Sam Nunn at hearings on Abuses in Federal Student Aid Programs in 1990, involved large-scale lending to students attending proprietary institutions.[10]

However, little appreciation for the political significance of the dollar volume of defaults likely to occur on loans made to students at vocational and proprietary schools existed on the part of the student loan industry in the late 1980s. Even Secretary of Education William Bennett, in a statement on 4 November 1987, appeared unwilling to blame proprietary schools for the emerging loan default problem.

Congress expanded loan eligibility significantly with the passage of the Education Amendments of 1980 (P.L. 96-374). In 1981, however, as part of the first Reagan budget, Congress imposed a need analysis on loans that temporarily slowed program growth. (See Postsecondary Student Assistance Amendments included in the Omnibus Budget Reconciliation Act of 1981, P.L. 97-35.) The 1981 budget resolution also contained ceilings in overall budget authority for the Department of Education that led to a reduction in the audit and program review capability of the department. This created the dilemma of reduced oversight capability at the department as loan volume grew. Proprietary school loans grew to approximately one-third of all student loans.

Poor policing of the proprietary school industry, both by the Department of Education and by accrediting bodies established by the proprietary school industry itself, may be blamed for planting the seeds of scandals that contributed to a general discrediting of the student loan program. However, an integral part of this development was a willingness of lenders to make loans to students at such schools regardless of the school's quality or default rate, a willingness of guaranty agencies to guaranty such loans, and a willingness of student loan secondary markets to provide financing.

By the late 1980s, the FFEL program was widely viewed as prone to abuse in the form of high defaults resulting from easy access to loans by students attending less-than-quality schools. FFEL also was plagued by excessive cost and complexity. Part of the motivation of Congress to "reform" FFEL was to address these concerns.[11]

How Congress Reacted to Problems in the Student Loan Program Prior to 1992

Congressional receptivity to the 1992 and 1993 direct lending proposals reflected, in part, an assumption that the FFEL program was subject to irreparable problems. For example, the program was described as "inordinately complex and cumbersome" by the GAO, which noted, "The Department's Office of Inspector General, the Office of Management and Budget, and our own reports have documented accountability problems that have contributed to defaults, fraud, and mismanagement."[12] These problems, as viewed by the Congress as it considered the 1992 amendments, fall into three categories: complexity, absence of financial integrity, and absence of safeguards for students from parties seeking to use the program to facilitate consumer fraud.

Complexity. Increasing congressional concern over student loan defaults and a desire to reduce the program's cost led to the FFEL program becoming extremely complex. The department also promulgated a series of increasingly complex rules and regulations. Actions taken include the November 1986 "due diligence" regulations designed to reduce defaults,[13] statutory requirements for multiple disbursement of loans to students, delayed disbursements of loans to first-year students, and limitations on interest billings. Each such action reduced the program's cost as promised but also rendered the program less and less comprehensible by members of the congressional authorizing committees and their staffs, let alone others. A consensus emerged that the program was more complex than necessary. Neither the student loan industry nor the higher education community was able to produce a regulatory relief package that was free from the criticism of further reducing the program's integrity.[14]

Some of the complexity in the program resulted from budget restraints that precluded opportunities for Congress to expand loan eligibility or otherwise enact new grant programs or provide significant new benefits to students. Other complexities resulted from the promulgation of arcane rules and regulations by the Department of Education to prevent recently identified program abuses from recurring.[15] Sometimes, in the opinion of the student loan industry, these rules and regulations failed to reflect even a cursory knowledge of loan servicing or data processing.

The dollar volume of defaults exploded between 1981 and 1991, reflecting the liberalized loan eligibility enacted in previous years and increases greater than inflation in higher education costs. According to the *GSL Data Book*, annual default claims paid to lenders increased from $257 million in FY 80 to $3.322 billion in FY 91. It is important to note that the rate of defaults remained basically constant throughout this period, a fact consistently de-emphasized by the Reagan and Bush Administrations. Increases in default costs were a reflection of the growth in loan volume.[16]

Absence of Financial Integrity. As loan volume and the federal budget deficit grew in the 1980s, all federal agencies sought to reduce costs by increasing accountability in programs within their jurisdiction. At the Department of Education, this effort took the form of new, detailed regulations governing the conduct of program participants. The new regulations changed the rules and procedures for loan servicing and collection, as well as other aspects of loan administration. The new rules were directed at ensuring competent loan administration, aggressive collection efforts on delinquent loans, and minimizing federal costs.[17] With the promulgation of new regulations, regulatory violations followed, leading to reports of "lender non-compliance" and suggestions that the program lacked financial integrity.

For most FFEL lenders, regulatory compliance was (and remains) a high priority. During the 1980s, however, two well-publicized incidents of regulatory non-compliance in loan servicing occurred, involving Florida Federal Savings and Loan and the California Student Loan Finance Corporation. The former resulted in eventual prosecution for fraud over falsified collection records.

The publicity surrounding these two incidents, continuing departmental concern about the program's financial integrity, and the insolvency of the largest of the guaranty agencies, the Higher Education Assistance Foundation (HEAF), contributed to ever-more-specific regulations and administrative requirements and a growing perception that the program was unmanageable.

Protection of Student-Consumers. Congressional concern over defaults crested in 1990 with the enactment of cohort default rate cutoffs for high-default-rate schools (P.L. 101-239). However, this action was undertaken to achieve budget savings, rather than to protect borrowers. As the 1980s ended (and since that time), congressional authorizing committees have remained reluctant to disenfranchise schools or otherwise place restrictions on the types of education supported by the federal student-aid programs.

Restrictions on institutional eligibility based on the student loan default rates is an imperfect solution to an unavoidable political − not policy − problem. Congress was caught in the dilemma of addressing defaults with this crude indicator of educational quality because development of a more accurate or fair measurement proved impossible.

By 1990, Senate Labor Committee Chairman Edward Kennedy (D-Mass.), opined that facilitating attendance of students at less-than-quality institutions was victimizing them, not helping them. Kennedy's and others' concerns led to increased congressional support for terminating the eligibility of high-default-rate institutions, clarifying the applicability of the Federal Trade Commission Holder Rule to student loans, and strengthening congressional oversight of accrediting bodies and state licensure agencies. (Some observers speculate that this trend will continue with closer scrutiny of the cost of higher education and, eventually, the imposition of price controls on institutions).

Loans to High-Risk Borrowers:
The Real Cause of the Program's Problems?

An understanding of the development of direct loans would be incomplete without identifying the failure of Congress to increase grant aid so as to preclude the need for student loans by lower-income students, which was the root cause of most of the problems of the FFEL program.[18] Put another way, had high-risk students been receiving grants rather than loans, there would not have been a significant default problem.

The failure of the higher education community to adequately support growth in the Pell grant and the campus-based programs is beyond the scope of this article. Even if an aggressive effort by the community had been undertaken, it might have failed. However, congressional attitudes toward student assistance changed as the program became complex and as efforts were undertaken to minimize the costs associated with defaults. As noted above, as the 1980s began, congressional support for the federal student-aid programs was strong. But as the media and consumer protection advocates' interest in defaults grew, so grew the concept of the student as a potential victim of the education system and the federal support programs.[19] Whether this would have occurred if grant aid had grown at the same rate as loans is open to question.

Once congressional attitudes toward student aid changed, a virtual cascade of reform proposals and actions followed. Part H (institutional integrity) of the 1992 Higher Education Act was the most comprehensive of these efforts. Some of the reforms, such as the required segregation of the trade association and accrediting commission functions, undertaken by single entities in the past, could lead to the collapse of some proprietary school associations.

Student-aid reform became an attractive political issue, perhaps best reflected in the 1990 oversight hearings of the Permanent Subcommittee on Investigations chaired by Senator Sam Nunn (D-Ga.). The committee focused on abuses in both the proprietary schools and student loan industry.

The souring of congressional attitudes toward the student loan program and the continuing efforts on the part of the Department of Education to prevent new program abuses likely would not have led to a fundamental restructuring of the student loan program, had not congressional budget procedures been altered in 1990. Instead, the process of piecemeal, incremental reform probably would have continued. However, the Credit Reform Act opened the door for a fundamental restructuring of the program and offered an opportunity to create the impression − if not the reality − that the problems inherent in providing loans to students for college were about to be solved.

Congressional Budget Procedure Changes: Did They Make the Direct Student Loan Program Inevitable?

Congress almost certainly would not have enacted direct loans in 1993 had it not first changed the congressional budget procedures relating to federal credit programs. These procedures were changed in October 1990, when congressional conferees on the Omnibus Budget Reconciliation of 1990 (P.L. 101-508) made a decision to include the Credit Reform Act (section 13201) in that legislation. This action was subject to little review or discussion by higher education or student loan policy experts. Developed largely through high level meetings between Bush Administration Office of Management and Budget (OMB) personnel and Congressional Budget Committee staff, credit reform was understood by few other members of Congress, relating as it did to the most esoteric aspects of congressional accounting procedures. It is unclear whether changes in budget scoring of the FFEL program were even a minor consideration of either congressional or Administration policymakers working on the proposal.[20]

The Credit Reform Act sought to more accurately reflect the costs associated with credit programs in the federal budget. Under the act, the full, life-of-the-loan cost of subsidies and insurance are recognized on present-value basis at the time the loan is made. This process contrasts with pre-1990 law, under which only current-year costs are recognized, not the future costs associated with the new loan commitments.

Pre-1990 budget procedures effectively discouraged serious consideration of fundamental student loan reform, such as the direct loan program. The altered budget scoring of credit programs reversed previous procedures under which 80% to 85% of loan costs appeared in subsequent fiscal budgets. Under pre-1990 procedures, the federal cost of student loans appeared to be lower than the actual cost of the entitlement commitments.[21]

The Credit Reform Act indisputably made budget scoring of federal credit programs, including direct and guaranteed student loans, more accurate. Unfortunately, the act contains its own scoring distortions, idiosyncrasies that make consideration of alternatives more difficult. These distortions include gross understatement of administrative costs and disregard for the full cost of new federal employees hired as a result of the new program.

The direct loan legislation − Federal Direct Student Loan Program (FDSLP) − is structured to minimize the recognized federal cost of the program. Under the legislation, the recognized cost to the government for loans is limited to the cost of funds, defaults, and a subset of actual administrative costs. The most widely recognized cost of the FFEL program, the "special allowance" interest subsidy paid to lenders and holders, does not appear in direct loans because the government is using its own funds, rather than "renting" private capital.

The Congressional Direct Loan Debate

As noted above, congressional concerns over the student loan program and the enactment of credit reform created an environment ready for change. What was lacking was a competent proposal for restructuring or replacing the program. Around 1990, such a proposal was put forward by Tom Butts of the University of Michigan. Butts developed a direct loan proposal based on a detailed knowledge of the structure of the existing student loan program and designed to eliminate lenders, guaranty agencies, and secondary markets from the process.

The Butts proposal initially received only lukewarm support among institutions. Persistent lobbying on his part, however, led to the emergence of a committed group of advocates who were excited by the prospect of simplifying loan administration through the removal of lenders and guaranty agencies from the student-aid arena.

The direct loan legislation, both as proposed and as ultimately enacted, only peripherally addresses the most pressing problem of the FFEL program — student loan defaults. The two main benefits of direct loans most often cited — program simplicity and reduced federal costs — have yet to be proven.[22]

In reviewing the direct loan debate, it is important to note that there were two major versions of student loan reform legislation, that proposed by Butts and Congressman Rob Andrews (D-N.J.) and that proposed by Congressman Thomas Petri (R-Wis.) and Senators Paul Simon (D-Ill.) and David Durenberger (R-Minn.). The latter (H.R. 2336) focused more on income-contingent repayment through the Internal Revenue Service (IRS) than on direct federal funding of loans. IRS collection of loans was opposed by some in the higher education community (including students) who otherwise supported direct lending. To maximize support for direct loans, however, the Petri approach was eventually blended into the Butts-Andrews approach as a servicing option.

While achieving savings from directly funding loans was discussed *ad nauseam*, the suggestion that savings could be used to increase grant aid quickly disappeared from the debate. Similarly, the claim of administrative simplicity was followed by an aggressive (and ultimately successful) campaign to secure an institutional administrative cost allowance. (An administrative allowance is provided for institutions under section 452(b) of the Higher Education Act.) As the results of the 1993 legislation unfold during implementation of the FDSLP, a student loan program is likely to appear that, from the student's perspective, looks remarkably like the former program.

The direct loan debate was subject to two major turning points. The first occurred when a significant number of educational institutions weighed in with concerns over the institutional burdens inherent in the program. The issues came in the form of letters to members of Congress.[23] Many of these letters expressed concerns about the institutional liability inherent in assuming a larger administrative role in the direct loan program or the cost of administering direct loans on campus. Many of the concerns were based on a detailed assessment of probable institutional costs using a cost-assessment model developed by the Student Loan Marketing Association.[24]

The second turning point in the direct loan debate was two papers published by the Congressional Research Service (CRS). The first was *Access to Student Loans and the Senate Proposal for Restructuring Under*

H.R. 2264, Congressional Research Service Report to Congress dated 19 July 1993, written by Dennis Zimmerman and Barbara Miles.[25] The second paper, *Guaranteed Student Loans Versus Direct Lending: Where Are the Savings?* established the credibility of the student loan industry claim that savings may be non-existent. The paper also found that, "Budget savings with shifting to direct lending are equally achievable by adjusting lender returns in the current program. Real economic savings would be achieved only if the government serviced and administered the program more efficiently than the private sector, a proposition subject to dispute." These assertions helped stimulate alternative change proposals.

The CRS papers' "independent" substantiation of the policy arguments of direct loan opponents led to a direct response by proponents. As expected, the direct loan proponents sought to rebut the paper by describing it as an academic overview by analysts with little experience in the Guaranteed Student Loan Program.

A major element of the campaign against direct loans took the form of a public relations effort by lenders, guaranty agencies, and secondary markets that was unprecedented. These efforts, many of which were undertaken by the Coalition for Student Loan Reform,[26] consisted of interviews with newspaper editorial boards, media appearances, and editorials. The effort was viewed as generally successful, resulting in well over a dozen media appearances, numerous editorials, and even some political cartoons.

While the student loan industry scrambled to substantiate the deficiencies in the official budget scoring of the Clinton proposal, the accuracy of the proposal was not questioned at the Department of Education or at the White House. The larger-than-anticipated, projected savings − $4.265 billion over five years − were the principal selling point of the entire proposal.

Chairman Ford took a similar position. Having decided to support the adoption of the new program, he showed little concern as to whether or not the savings were real. What Ford saw was the possibility of meeting a stiff reconciliation instruction while not reducing assistance to college students. The new program was money without pain.

Most House committee Republicans, led by Congressman Bill Goodling (R-Pa.), opposed the plan and were sympathetic to the doubts cast on the budget savings. However, these members had no intention of simply not complying with the reconciliation instruction. Instead, they believed the program needed to be trimmed back; the subsidies paid to lenders, guaranty agencies, and secondary markets needed to be reduced. The student loan industry had no choice but to acquiesce and support this effort.

The subsidy cuts proposed in the Senate bill triggered concerns that loan access to high-risk borrowers could be jeopardized or that guaranty agency insolvencies could be precipitated. The CRS paper, *Access to Student Loans and the Senate Proposal for Restructuring Under H.R. 2264*, addressed these issues. This paper analyzed the impact on specified lenders of the changes proposed by the Senate and suggested that disproportionately deep cuts were being made to the Student Loan Marketing Association. The paper concluded that the subsidy cuts could adversely affect the availability of loans to students, especially those in short-term courses of study.

The package of subsidy cuts prepared by the Senate and various House members reflected little input from the student loan community. This resulted from the inability of the industry to speak with one voice. The loudest voice within the student loan industry was that of Sallie Mae. Unfortunately, it had no intention of developing reform proposals as part of a committee. Instead, it internally developed a set of proposals designed to inflict minimal damage to its earnings while creating new market opportunities to make up for the damage in volume. The principal features of the Sallie Mae proposal were the use of an auction to determine lender yield and a 5% reduction in the insurance paid to lenders on defaults. Notwithstanding the fact that Sallie Mae itself was ineligible to participate in the auction, it was uniquely positioned to dominate the auction process by providing advice and other assistance to bidders who intended to sell their loans to it. Similarly, risk sharing was easy for Sallie Mae to accept because it could compensate for the risk through the price it offered to the seller.

As the legislative process continued, more than one attempt was made to find common ground with Sallie Mae; but no agreement was ever reached. Even as Sallie Mae went through the motions of discussing alternative means of achieving program savings, it was advocating its own proposals in congressional offices.

The ultimate failure to develop a consensus community position with which to combat the Clinton proposal occurred despite unusual direct assistance from a member of Congress. Congressman Bart Gordon (D-Tenn.), with help from Representatives Goodling and Earl Pomeroy (D-N.D.), injected himself into the student loan debate and undertook a painstaking effort to achieve a student loan industry consensus. The

Gordon-Goodling-Pomeroy effort included actively participating in meetings with banks, guaranty agencies, secondary markets, and Sallie Mae, at which the development of a consensus package was attempted. But the effort failed largely because of Sallie Mae's refusal to accept any package containing a user fee on its holdings or new financing. (The Gordon effort did lead to a package of proposed FFEL program savings, which was introduced as H.R. 2219 on 20 May 1993.)

Occurring simultaneously with the Gordon-Goodling-Pomeroy effort were bipartisan discussions among Senate authorizing committee staff, principally the staffs of Senators Pell, Jeffords, and Kassebaum. All three Senators were opposed to full implementation of direct loans but were uncertain about how the proposal could be defeated. The unexpected support of the student loan industry for subsidy cuts led to a strategy under which cost reductions to borrowers would be offered as an alternative to the direct loan bill. A package of massive cuts in the loan origination fee and insurance premium were adopted, all paid for with deeper cuts in lender special allowances and the imposition of new fees on lenders.

Ultimately, the Pell-Kassebaum strategy worked, as several moderate members of the conference committee supported the compromise that adopted both a large direct loan program and the substantial benefits to borrowers.

The "Ugly" Conference Committee of 1993

There is no congressional rule of procedure requiring rationality to govern the conduct of conference committees between the House and Senate. Had there been such a rule, the conference on the student loan provisions of the 1993 budget reconciliation act might have been ruled out of order. The conduct of the conference committee on the legislation precluded any opportunity for the student loan industry (or anyone else) to offer meaningful input to the conferees on whether the dramatic reductions in subsidies paid to lenders and guarantors in the FFEL program left a viable program in place.

The conference committee brought together all of the emotions of a struggling new Administration looking for enactment of at least part of its domestic policy agenda (regardless of its merits), an embattled industry, and a group of ideologically motivated higher education lobbyists. The aggressive challenge of Congressman William D. Ford by Congressman Bart Gordon served as a catalyst to fully ignite what otherwise might have proved to be a difficult but basically orderly conference.

Gordon, an energetic Democrat from Tennessee, had proved himself to be an able opponent of Chairman Ford well before the 1993 conference. During consideration of the 1992 reauthorization, Gordon took the floor to suggest that the Education and Labor Committee had favored proprietary school owners over the students recruited to attend such schools.

Gordon, convinced the direct loan program was a mistake, sought to block enactment of the program. Initially, working with Congressman Goodling and others, he sought to develop an alternative to direct loans by incorporating subsidy reductions equal to the savings requirements of the 1993 budget resolution. As discussed above, this effort failed because of the inability of the student loan industry to rally behind a single proposal. Then Gordon and Goodling tried to document the opposition of House members to the legislation incorporated into the omnibus reconciliation bill. They were successful, but the effort said more about the reconciliation process than about any aspect of the direct loans.

Gordon and Goodling secured the signatures of 239 members on a letter directed to the conferees on the student loan portions of the reconciliation bill.[27] Each signature represented a questioning of a small part of the Clinton program and the ease with which the House Education and Labor Committee had federalized a $26 billion-a-year loan program.

When the letter reached Chairman Ford, he rejected it out of hand. Ford, indifferent to the position of a majority of his colleagues, rejected the Gordon-Goodling effort as irrelevant to the resolution of conference differences.

The hostile environment also prevented any effort to review the subsidy cuts, which could have improved the conference agreement. During this conference process the Clinton Administration showed little inclination to assure Congress that enactment would balance the concerns of direct loan opponents with its own interest in appearing to enact a major change in student loan policy. The resulting final legislation, the work of Chairman Ford more than anyone else, reflects the haphazardness of a legislative battle characterized more by political passion than thoughtful deliberation. The outcomes are as follows:

1. Financial support paid to or received by guaranty agencies was dramatically reduced. Examples include reduction of the maximum insurance premium from 3% to 1%, no restrictions on the selection of schools into the direct loan program (regardless of the impact on any particular guaranty agency), and enactment

of dramatic authority over agency reserve funds. The cumulative impact of these changes could be to precipitate the insolvency of one or more agencies, thereby jeopardizing the availability of loans to students.

2. Interest subsidies to lenders were sharply reduced (for the most part on loans made after 1 July 1995), creating a high probability of loan access problems for high-risk student borrowers. Last-minute attempts during the process to review subsidy cuts to minimize any negative effect on students were stymied by the nature of the conference process.

3. Direct loan provisions were enacted with very little specificity, as congressional Democrats responded to Administration desires to leave open as many details as possible. The result is a program that will become fully known only after the regulations for it are implemented (some without notice and comment).

All of the above can hardly be described as sound education policymaking.

Direct Loan Policy Advocacy:
A Student Loan Industry Perspective

Several months after President Clinton signed the reconciliation bill, many in the student loan industry still have difficulty understanding why Congress enacted a direct government loan program. The answer may lie in the changing politics of the budget deficit. To a person, those most involved in the student loan debate focused on loan-specific issues, rather than the overall budget process. This was not without reason. Even at $4 billion, student loan savings were too small to merit much attention, despite the attempts by Representatives Gordon and Goodling; and the savings claimed for direct loans were too large to be eliminated from the legislation, regardless of how questionable the estimates were proved to be.[28]

The pro-direct loan advocates had powerful allies both in the Clinton Administration and on Capitol Hill. Most influential inside the Administration was Deputy Secretary Madeleine Kunin, who eagerly picked up the issue and pursued it with a campaign-like fervor. On Capitol Hill, Senator Simon missed few opportunities for promoting the program.[29] Mailings were sent out to sizable mailing lists and, on at least one occasion, fax messages were sent to colleges urging them to contact committee members to demand the enactment of the program.

The Simon efforts and efforts of various other direct loan proponents raise serious questions about the extent to which members of Congress or congressional committee staff should be involved in generating grass-roots support for programs in the committees on which they serve. No laws were broken. However, the student loan industry considered it hypocritical for some congressional direct loan proponents to criticize industry lobbying efforts when they themselves were undertaking much larger efforts in their offices, using federal funds or the threat of exclusion from the policymaking process.

In some respects the sizable public relations efforts mounted by the industry backfired. The vehemence of school proponents of direct government lending increased in proportion to industry opposition. Some association-based advocates became heroes to some of their peers for "standing up" to the well-heeled student loan industry's public relations efforts.

The outreach of the student loan industry to institutions during the debate was never really successful. Most advocacy for direct loans was promoted through the presidential associations. But most lender and guaranty agency contacts with schools were with financial-aid administrators, not presidents. Banks and others knew few higher education leaders directly, and the middle of the direct loan debate presented a poor opportunity to develop contacts and relationships.

Outreach to schools took several forms. First, a number of program participants developed informative, professionally edited newsletters containing information about the direct loan issue. *The Report*, a newsletter published by the Coalition for Student Loan Reform, is an example. Second, meetings were held where information was shared on the problems likely to be caused by direct loans. Third, direct loan opponents at institutions were encouraged to communicate directly with Congress.

A really successful argument against direct government loans was never developed. It is questionable if such an argument was even possible. The argument that direct lending did not save money missed the point for many aid officers and colleges; they accepted the representations of Butts and others that the new program would be easier to administer. The argument that the Department of Education could not run the program rang true to many schools, but it was essentially a negative argument. The enthusiasm and promises of the new Clinton appointees at the Department of Education met the concerns of many schools. The opponents' argument that a transition to direct loans could result in student loans not being available was labeled successfully as a "scare tactic" by direct loan proponents.[30] Many schools accepted the risk of loans not being available as inherent in any federal student loan program, including the existing one.

The most credible arguments against direct government loans came not from the industry but from a small group of financial-aid administrators who either supported the current program or fundamentally distrusted the department. Among these leaders were Joe Russo of the University of Notre Dame, Tom Rutter of the University of California-San Diego, Jim Belvin of Duke University, and representatives of various historically black colleges and universities. These schools put out a simple but convincing plea that they did not want to assume the new responsibilities inherent in direct loans.[31]

The anti-direct loan posture on the part of some schools and the quiet but substantial distrust of others led to the National Association of Student Financial Aid Administrators (NASFAA) taking an equivocal position on the new program. A June 1993 NASFAA survey reported that 10% of respondents favored a phase-in of the direct lending program to replace FFEL. Fifty-four percent favored a parallel direct lending demonstration program to evaluate the effectiveness of direct loans before pushing out FFEL. However, only 2% indicated that they intended to participate in the demonstration program. Thirty-six percent favored retaining the FFEL program.

Change for the Sake of Change

The direct loan program is likely to produce few, if any, benefits for either students or schools. Those few benefits that will occur are byproducts of efforts against the direct loan program. However, this has not prevented the Administration from taking credit for reducing borrower interest rates or origination fees. The administrative simplicity promised for direct loans is fast disappearing as the realities of establishing an administrative structure for the new program set in. Similarly, the benefits students hoped for have not been realized and are more remote than ever, given the continued budget deficit. In this sense, the enactment of the Federal Direct Student Loan Program must be interpreted as an expression of congressional desire to *appear* to be expanding federal student assistance under difficult budget conditions.

That reducing the cost of student loans was not the prime objective is best evidenced in the categorical rejection by the Committee on Education and Labor and others of a proposal under which federal funds would be forwarded to existing program participants as an alternative to enacting the direct loan program. Under such a system, federal liability resulting from student default could have been dramatically limited, while at the same time avoiding the $500 million-plus start up costs of the new program.

The most lasting effect of the 1993 legislation on federal student assistance is likely to be the destruction of the FFEL program and the yet-to-be-determined federal bailout cost. Within three years, a sufficient number of guaranty agencies, lenders, and secondary markets will withdraw from the program, making a restoration of the FFEL program impossible. Any revival of a guaranty-based system is likely to involve a finite number of lenders contracting with the Department of Education and using one or more guaranty agencies as agents of the federal government operating at a higher volume than under current law.

The desire to restructure student aid could spell a troubled future for other federal education programs. The Pell grant program, in particular, could be the next target of "reform."[32]

Conclusion

The 1993 legislative process suggests that Clinton Administration eagerness to achieve a domestic policy change, coupled with the acquiescence of a large part of the higher education community to such change, led to a restructuring of federal higher education finance policy that may be described as anything but carefully planned. The byproduct of this effort was the dismantlement of a program that had largely lost its political credibility as a result of repeated abuses and reckless expansion of student and school eligibility. Only time will tell whether permanent harm to educational opportunity will result. It already is clear that no real progress or improvement in federal student assistance occurred.

In an ideal world, the chairs of congressional authorizing committees would exercise better stewardship over the programs in their jurisdictions. They would be immune to the politics that lead to hasty, haphazard policymaking. The House committee's conduct of the legislative process, as well as the tendency of the Clinton Administration to embrace a proposal before ever understanding it, is a model of how higher education policy should *not* be developed. However, a fundamental change in the nature of Congress or politics in general is not likely.

Footnotes

1. Loans authorized under part D of Title IV of the Higher Education Act as amended: Under the direct loan program, education institutions originate loans as agents

of the federal government, and all loan servicing is performed by outside contractors. There is nothing "direct" about direct loans as far as the nexus between the borrower and the federal government is concerned. Loans authorized under part B of Title IV of the Higher Education Act of 1965, as amended: The program was known as the Guaranteed Student Loan Program (GSLP) until its name was changed to the Federal Family Education Loan Program (FFELP) in the Higher Education Amendments of 1992 (Public Law 102-325). The program will be referred to as the Federal Family Education Loan Program or FFELP throughout this paper, including references to the program prior to the name change.

2. The Education Amendments of 1976 (P.L. 94-482) significantly increased federal support for the establishment and operation of guaranty agencies. As early as FY 71, loan guaranty volume in the guaranty agency-based program exceeded that of the FISL program. Since FY 85, no new guarantees have been made under FISL. U.S. Department of Education, *Guaranteed Student Loan Programs Data Book, FY 91* (Washington, D.C., 1992).

3. A detailed description of how the Federal Direct Student Loan Program is likely to work was included in the committee report accompanying H.R. 3553, the Higher Education Amendments of 1993, pp. 57-66. The Department of Education also has released a "Fact Sheet" description of the program.

4. Thomas A. Butts and Elizabeth M. Hicks, "The Direct Lending Debate, Making the Case for and Dispelling Myths About Direct Lending," *NACUBO Business Officer* (February 1992).

5. The potential increased liabilities were discounted by direct loan proponents during the debate. Since the program was enacted, institutions have sponsored additional research in this area. See the memorandum of White, Verville, Fulton, and Saner, prepared for the American Council on Education, "Potential Sources." This memorandum attempts to definitively identify institutional liabilities under the Federal Direct Student Loan Program. Also see "Comments on White, Verville, Fulton and Saner Memorandum on Potential Sources of Liability to Institutions Participating in the Federal Direct Student Loan Program (FDSLU)," November 1993, prepared by Clohan & Dean.

6. Arthur Hauptman, *The Tuition Dilemma: Assessing New Ways to Pay for College* (Washington, D.C.: Brookings Institution, 1990). Hauptman notes, "The average annual increase in college tuitions from 1980 to 1987 was about 10%, whereas the price index for food and new cars rose at 4% a year and the median price of a new house grew at 7%." See also "Making College Affordable Again," the final report of the Commission on Responsibilities for Financing Postsecondary Education. The report notes that "from 1980 to 1990, attendance costs at public institutions rose 109% — or an average annual rate of 8% — while at private institutions attendance costs increased 146%, or about 10% annually" (p. 4).

7. U.S. Department of Education, *Guaranteed Student Loan Programs Data Book, FY 91* (Washington, D.C., 1992), p. 16.

8. Ibid., p. 24.

9. College Board, *Trends in Student Aid: 1983 to 1993* (Washington, D.C., 1993), p. 9.

10. "Hearings Before the Permanent Subcommittee on Investigations of the Committee on Governmental Affairs, United States Senate," *Abuses in Federal Student-Aid Programs*, S.Hrg. 101-659 (Washington, D.C.: U.S. Government Printing Office, 1990).

11. See "U.S. House of Representatives, 102d Congress, 2d Session, Higher Education Amendments of 1992," *Report of the Committee on Education and Labor* (Washington, D.C.: U.S. Government Printing Office, 1992). The report notes, "In addition to being more expensive than direct loans, the Committee believes that the current Stafford Student Loan program suffers from a number of problems, as documented in the May 1991 report of the Senate Permanent Subcommittee on Investigations, chaired by Senator Sam Nunn. These problems include: a high rate of student defaults, financial failure of one major guarantee agency, questions about the strength and number of guarantee agencies, severe problems in managing student loans by lenders, and fraud and abuse by certain lenders and some trade schools" (p. 59).

12. U.S. General Accounting Office, *Transition Series: Education Issues*, GAO/OCG-93-18TR (Washington, D.C., 1992).

13. 34 C.F.R. 682.411, promulgated November 1986.

14. See, as examples, the recommendations of the Consumer Bankers Association for the reauthorization of the Higher Education Act, reprinted in "U.S. House of Representatives, 102d Congress, 1st Session, Hearings on the Reauthorization of the Higher Education Act of 1965: Stafford Loans: Hearings before the Subcommittee on Postsecondary Education of the Committee on Education and Labor," pp. 46-50, and the statement of Lawrence A. Hough, President and Chief Executive Officer, Student Loan Marketing Association, in the same report.

15. The detailed "due diligence" regulations promulgated in 1986 as 34 C.F.R. 682.411 precipitated a crisis in the student loan program that led to the promulgation, by administrative bulletin, of "cure procedures," under which disallowed default claims could be restored to insurance eligibility. See "Dear Colleague" letter G138, dated March 1988.

16. "U.S. Senate, 102d Congress, 1st Session, Reauthorizing the Higher Education Act of 1965," *Report of the Committee on Labor and Human Resources, United States Senate to Accompany S. 1150* S. Rpt. 102-204 (Washington, D.C.: U.S. Government Printing Office, 1991), p. 5.

17. See November 1986 regulations, *Federal Register*, Vol. 51, No. 217, pp. 40886-40947.

18. Much has been written on the loan-grant imbalance. See "U.S. Senate, 102d Congress, 1st Session, Reauthorizing the Higher Education Act of 1965," *Report of the Committee on Labor and Human Resources, United States Senate, to Accompany S. 1150* (Washington, D.C.: U.S. Government Printing Office, 1991). "The implication of the decline in the purchasing power of the Pell grant is clear: needy students have no choice but to turn to loans. . . . Directing Federally guaranteed loans to borrowers at the highest risk of default is a contradictory and self-defeating policy and we are seeing its results in the $3.6 billion in default costs we will pay this year" (p. 6).

19. See, for example, the testimony of Clarence C. Crawford, Associate Director, Education and Employment Issues, Human Resources Division, General Accounting Office, before the Subcommittee on Human Resources and Intergovernmental Relations, Committee on Government Operations, 10 June 1993. Crawford noted, "The lure of plentiful financial aid for proprietary school students, and the abusive practices of some proprietary schools – including fraud – has had a disproportionate impact on defaults."

20. Charlotte Fraas, *Federal Family Education Loans: Issues Relating to a Change to Direct Loans*, Congressional Research Service Report for Congress (Washington, D.C.: CRS, Library of Congress, 1993).

21. For purposes of this paper, references to the "student loan community" or "student loan industry" are references to eligible lenders participating in the student loan program, guaranty agencies, tax-exempt and other secondary markets, and the government-sponsored enterprise established to support liquidity in the student loan program, the Student Loan Marketing Association (Sallie Mae).

22. The General Accounting Office, among others, would disagree with this contention. A series of GAO reports to Congress helped "prove" direct loans would save "billions." Among these reports are: U.S. General Accounting Office, *Student Loans: Direct Loans Could Save Money and Simplify Program Administration*, GAO/HRD-91-144BR (Washington, D.C., 1991); and U.S. General Accounting Office, *Student Loans: Direct Loans Could Save Billions in First 5 Years with Proper Implementation*, GAO/HRD-93-27 (Washington, D.C., 1992).

   A different view is presented in Rudolph G. Penner, *Direct Government Lending vs. Guarantees for Student Loans: A Comparative Analysis* (Washington, D.C.: KPMG Peat Marwick, 1992). The Congressional Budget Office itself indicated savings would be significantly below the $4.265 billion over five years in the official estimate in a letter to Senator Claiborne Pell dated 26 May 1993. The letter indicated that when all administrative costs associated with direct loans were taken into consideration, savings fell to $2.08 billion over five years.

23. USA Group, Inc. produced a compendium of letters to members of Congress and association resolutions titled, "The Groundswell of Concern About Direct Government Lending: Submitted to the Senate Committee on Labor and Human Resources." The compilation includes more than 100 letters from schools expressing various concerns over direct loans.

24. See *Direct Lending Impact Evaluation Model: Institution Assessment Guide*, April 1993, prepared by the Student Loan Marketing Association.

25. See also, memorandum of Barbara Miles and Dennis Zimmerman to Bart Gordon on achieving competitive returns and reducing costs in the guaranteed student loan program, dated 23 April 1993.

26. The Coalition for Student Loan Reform was established in 1993 for the purpose of promoting student loan reform as an alternative to direct lending. Members included nonprofit education loan organizations. The group is chaired by Dr. Dan Cheever of American Student Assistance, Inc.

27. The Gordon-Goodling letter noted the 397 to 28 vote on a Gordon amendment to the Labor-HHS-Education Appropriations bill for FY 94, which placed a limit

on administrative expenses for direct loans for FY 94. The letter also noted, "In February of this year economists at the Congressional Research Service (CRS) concluded that '[c]onversion to direct loans cannot be justified on the basis of either budget savings or increases in overall economic welfare'."

28. It is important to note that most early estimates of the budget impact of a direct loan program suggested significant budget savings. See, for example, *Student Loans: Direct Loans Could Save Money and Simplify Program Administration*, GAO/HRD-91-144BR (Washington, D.C.: General Accounting Office, September 1991). Early reports included those issued by the General Accounting Office and the CBO itself. By the time the first credible alternative estimates were available, the assumption of more than $4.2 billion over five years through enactment of direct loans had been incorporated into the budget resolution.

29. Typical of Simon's efforts were the "press packet" and press conference he called in response to the "lobby day" called by the Consumer Bankers Association. The press release issued by Simon described the lobby day as an attempt "to try to smother in the cradle the proposed direct student loan plan." The press kit, issued by Simon's press secretary, informs the press that, "Simon has worked behind the scenes for months to convince the President and his advisors to reach this decision [to support direct loans] and deserves great credit for steady and stunning progress in advancing this issue, against great initial odds and entrenched special interests." The statement also describes the Clinton Administration's proposed legislation as "Simon's plan," even though it differed dramatically from that proposed by Simon (IDEA Credit), which was itself the Senate version of legislation developed by Rep. Thomas Petri (R-Wis.). All of Simon's activities were carried out from his Senate or Senate Committee offices, using federally paid employees.

30. See "Facts and Myths About Direct Loans," produced by the U.S. Department of Education. This document was sent, at taxpayer expense, to the department's mailing list of Title IV participating schools.

31. See the letter of John L. Henderson, President of Wilberforce University, to Honorable David Hobson, dated 29 April 1993. Henderson notes, "I know that you take seriously the need for cost savings in all federal programs, just as we do at Wilberforce. However, the costs associated with a direct government loan program would run counter to our current efforts to streamline administrative costs. In order for Wilberforce to administer a direct government loan program, we would have to hire an estimated 4 additional staff at $100,000 based on our current salary rates." Many of the institutional concerns expressed in letters to Congress were based on an assessment of institutional cost using a model developed by the Student Loan Marketing Association (Sallie Mae). Although the Sallie Mae model was assailed by some direct loan supporters as creating a biased picture of institutional cost, the conclusion of many institutions, that institutional costs would significantly increase, was never effectively rebutted by direct loan proponents on or off Capitol Hill.

32. A discouraging sign is the fact that the Senate Permanent Subcommittee on Investigations of the Committee on Governmental Affairs has started hearings into the Pell grant program. The first of the hearings was held on November 1993.

PART III
COMMENTARY

Two Tough Battles, Two New Laws: What Can We Learn from All of This?

By John F. Jennings

The new national community service program and the reform of the student loan programs were the major education legislation of the first year of the Clinton Administration. Even though the community service legislation encompassed support for a range of activities from high school service learning to older American volunteer programs, these two laws were conceptually tied together. For instance, the new student loan program included an option for repayment pegged to the income level of the individual, thereby encouraging college graduates to take lower-paying jobs that would be of benefit to their communities. It was also advantageous to link the cutbacks in the costs of student loan programs to the creation of a major community service initiative.

This book's 10 essays on these two topics may leave the reader a bit confused about the amount of agreement that existed in the nation's capital as these two laws were being fashioned. As might be expected, the proponent writers, whether in the Administration, Congress, or private groups, strongly assert the correctness of the policies that were adopted; but their assuredness is matched in intensity by the writers who opposed these programs.

This series of books is fashioned so that all the major points of view can be known; therefore, advocates and skeptics are both afforded the opportunity to express their opinions. However, the key fact that must be remembered is that the proponents of community service and of direct lending prevailed. Their ideas became the law of the land. Whether these particular policies are sustained over time is another question; but for now, the President and his allies have won.

But it is useful for those curious about public policy to read all of these different points of view. When a major decision is made, the certainty of that policy is not always evident. Only the historians have the luxury of looking back and saying that, of course, a decision was correct. Knowing all the various arguments and counter-arguments, therefore, helps one to better appreciate the tenor of the time of the decision making and the reasons for certain compromises.

It is also helpful to know where people are coming from when they advocate certain ideas. For instance, many Democrats prefer to carry out policy by creating a federal program to achieve it, while many Republicans are adverse to the federal government undertaking any initiative. It also is useful to know whether groups outside the government gain financially from the concepts that they propose. Thus, in reading these essays, one must attend to the arguments and be alert to the philosophical bents and the financial interests of the writers.

This book could not include all of the players. Rather, it concentrates on the major controversies and the major actors in those disputes. Consequently, some aspects of the decision making are not covered. For instance, in the community service bill, the amendments offered in the House by opponents of the legislation are not discussed in depth. Nor, in the direct lending bill, is the Senate consideration of various proposals explored in detail. Readers must go to other sources for this information.

In the next several pages I will discuss some of the lessons that can be learned from the major disputes. For the sake of convenience, I group this information according to those aspects of the bills that involved the Clinton Administration, the Congress, and, finally, groups and individuals outside the government.

Administration

When Eli Segal and others in the new Clinton Administration sat down to write the community service bill, they faced the task of converting a broad campaign promise into a specific federal program. This was not an easy job.

As Senator Kassebaum points out in her paper, Clinton had talked during the campaign about establishing a National Trust Fund "to guarantee every American who wants a college education the means to obtain one." She also remarks that some estimates put the first-year costs of this concept at $7.5 billion. The legislation that was submitted to Congress cost much less than this amount because the Administration could not find the funds to pay for it; therefore, the program was less comprehensive than first proposed during the campaign. The final bill signed into law by the President cost even less because it had to be pared back even further in order to achieve enactment.

The campaign promise collided with the reality of the budgetary and political situation in Washington. Some observers will say that Clinton broke the promise by not following through on what he said during the campaign. Others will say that Clinton's campaign set out a vision of what he hoped to do; but when he assumed office, he had to reconcile that vision with fiscal reality.

It might be helpful to remember the context of the times. During his term in office, President Bush was accused of not having a vision for America. Commentators said that all he cared about was foreign affairs and that he could not articulate what he wanted the federal government to do to revitalize the country by dealing with its social and economic problems.

To show his difference from Bush, Clinton gave his vision of how he wanted to use the national government to address the nation's problems; therefore, he presented many ideas, including a national community service concept. He talked in grand terms about the thousands of young people who could be encouraged to help their communities, and he spoke broadly about how such service could help these youth to pay for a college education.

Then, when he assumed office, he met reality in trying to put into legislation all the elements of his "vision for America." So maybe the first lesson that we can glean from the transformation of the community service idea as a campaign promise to its realization as a program is that campaign promises show the general direction that a candidate will take, rather than serve as a precise guide for subsequent action.

The second lesson is as important as the first, and probably less obvious: The budget deficit drives policymaking in Washington. No major decision is made without fitting it into the perceived reality of the growing national debt. For example, the community service idea was scaled back because the Administration could not find the money to pay for it.

Conversely (some would say perversely), the reform of the student loan programs was made possible by a change in the accounting system used by the federal government to figure out the costs of its actions. Despite differences on other issues, all the papers on the student loan program agree on one thing: Direct lending could not have been enacted in any way without the Credit Reform Act of 1990. Those loans operated the same way before 1990 as they did afterward, but the federal government counted them as costing less after 1990 because of this change in accounting. Therefore, the rules of the federal budget process helped to determine national policy.

The last lesson to be learned from the Administration's formulation of policy in these two areas is that any president's job is easier if the Congress is of the same party. Neither President Reagan in his second term nor President Bush in his only term had that luxury. Whenever they proposed any legislation, the tendency was for the Democrats in Congress to be suspicious. President Clinton did not have a smooth relationship with Congress in his first year in office, but he achieved most of his goals because there was some loyalty toward him by the members of his own party – and they controlled the legislature.

Eli Segal and others involved in writing the community service bill nurtured this loyalty by consulting with the Democrats in Congress as they drafted the legislation. Senator Kennedy, for instance, proudly mentions this advice-seeking in his paper. On the other hand, Senator Kassebaum pointedly remarks that the Republicans were not consulted until the bill was finished; and this may have had some effect on the attitude of the minority party toward that legislation.

It is a tricky business for any Administration to know when to consult with Congress. If the same party controls both the Administration and the Congress, then it is best to try to keep close ties with the legislative leadership, since they will be asked to carry the President's program. But now and then, an Administration will not have the same ideas as the members of its own party in the Congress. For instance, with respect to the direct lending proposal, Congressman Ford, who chairs the committee in the House, was in accord with the Clinton Administration on the issue; but Senator Claiborne Pell, chair of the subcommittee on education in the Senate, was very skeptical of the proposal.

When it comes to members of the party different from the Administration in power, the President usually must try to consult them, but not if it means that his own party members will be angered because he is going to the other party. Yet if he does not talk with the other party, then he loses any chance of them helping him to achieve his goals.

In sum, the lessons to be learned from these two bills with regard to the executive branch are that any Administration must balance many competing interests when it fashions its program. A President must try to fulfill his campaign promises, even if he cannot do so fully. A President also must try to stay close to the members of his own party, even if they do not always share the same ideas. Further, even with the difficulties of reaching agreement within a party, it is easier to govern with one party in control of the executive and legislative branches than it is when there is a divided government. And last and very important, the federal budget deficit is an overarching concern in current policymaking in Washington; and no President can ignore it when he fashions his programs.

Congress

The adage is that the President proposes, but the Congress disposes. It is true that the Congress must pass any legislation for it to become law, and therefore the legislature is very important in our constitutional scheme. The President is not inconsequential, however, in that he generally establishes the agenda for the Congress and uses the powers of his Administration to influence its actions. Therefore, law making is a shared responsibility.

As already mentioned, this system often works better when the executive and the legislature are of the same party. Since our country has a strong tradition of two political parties, there tends to be greater tension when control of the government is divided between the parties. One party is always afraid that the other will gain an advantage, and so one party tries to find fault in the other's proposals. The positive in this fault-finding in that it keeps both parties on their toes; but it does impede decision making.

Even if the government is controlled by the same party, the path is not always clear. There frequently is tension within a party as to the best course of action, and members do not agree at all times.

The first six months of the Clinton Administration were tense all the way around. The new President and his team were inexperienced; but nonetheless, they established an ambitious agenda for action, including dealing with many very difficult issues, especially the budget deficit.

The Democrats fought some battles among themselves, but they were able to maintain their unity and generally supported the goals of the Clinton Administration. Their problem was that they were cocky after regaining the Presidency, and so they tried to pass legislation with only Democratic support and did not try hard to reach compromises and secure votes from the Republicans.

The Republicans, in turn, were disappointed about losing the Presidency and were searching for the proper positions to allow themselves to regain power. For example, they would not negotiate with the Democrats on any budget-deficit package containing new taxes because they wanted to paint the Democrats as the party of burdensome taxation.

185

Since the most important legislation of the first seven months of 1993 dealt with deficit reduction, all of these partisan considerations made the atmosphere tense and acrimonious. These feelings filled the air and affected all the legislation being considered, even if it did not deal directly with the budget. Senators Kennedy and Kassebaum and Representatives Ford and Goodling all allude to these partisan feelings and the general mood in Washington. The Republicans did not want to give the new President any easy victories, and the Democrats were trying hard to show that they could deliver after 12 years of government control divided between the two parties.

Thus the first lesson to be drawn from the congressional consideration of these two issues is that the general atmosphere of the times affects legislation. This lesson is easy to forget, because histories tend to be written about individual actions and seldom consider the environment in which those actions were taken.

Another important lesson is that the form in which legislation is presented can have serious consequences for the decisions made on the issues. The community service bill was dealt with as a regular bill, which meant that it went through the process open to amendment at many different points (and also open to filibuster in the Senate). By contrast, the direct lending proposal was made part of the budget reconciliation bill, which meant that the possibility for amendments and filibusters was sharply limited.

"Reconciliation" is an important term because it involves a relatively new means of enacting legislation that often has been employed during the last 13 years to establish important policies. In the 1970s the Congress adopted a congressional reform that sought to enable broad decision making on money matters. The concern then was that the various appropriations and tax bills were being enacted individually, and Congress never addressed the larger questions of raising and allocating tax revenues. Consequently, the adoption of an annual budget resolution was required, and the passage of a bill "reconciling" other legislation to this budget resolution was permitted.

These budget resolutions did not have any major effects in the 1970s, and reconciliation was rarely used. But in 1981 the new Republican Administration used these procedures to carry out the Reagan program of cuts in the domestic budget, increases in military spending, and decreases in taxes. David Stockman, who had served in the Congress and then became Reagan's budget director, realized that budget reconciliation had the potential to be a major policy instrument for bringing together many different decisions into one package. In the House of Representatives the rules could be used to limit opposition to a reconciliation bill by permitting only one "up-or-down" vote. And in the Senate the reconciliation bill carrying out the budget resolution could not be filibustered. Therefore, Reagan's entire program was adopted after a few votes; and obstructionist tactics were unsuccessful.

Clinton often stated that he admired the way Reagan got the Congress to adopt his program in 1981, although Clinton did not agree philosophically with all of the policies. So in 1993, after assuming office, Clinton worked with the Democratic leadership in the Congress to fold as many decisions as possible into the budget resolution and then into the reconciliation bill carrying out that resolution. Due to the "up-or-down" vote in the House and the lack of a filibuster in the Senate, he was able to achieve enactment of his budget-deficit reduction even though it contained many unpopular items.

The importance of this procedure to our understanding of the direct loan issue is that the reform was accomplished through the budget resolution and the reconciliation bill. Because of the peculiar rules surrounding these procedures, bankers, state guaranty agencies, and secondary loan markets — although they spent considerable money and effort fighting these changes — were not able to break into the decision-making process.

Congressman Ford, chairman of the House committee, was a strong advocate of these changes; and once he convinced his committee to support the reforms, that decision was final because the bill could not be amended on the floor of the House. Moreover, since the chairman of a committee has considerable influence over who gets appointed to Senate-House conference committees, Congressman Ford was able to dominate the House side of the conference committee that was convened to decide the final form of the legislation. Both Congressman Goodling and John Dean make clear in their papers how frustrated they were that Chairman Ford was able to be so strong on this issue even when, they contend, his views were not those of a majority of the House.

The point is that it makes a crucial difference whether a bill goes through the ordinary legislative process or is folded into the reconciliation bill. Form can determine outcome.

The last lesson to be learned from the congressional consideration of community service and student loans is that many issues become interconnected in the legislative process. President Clinton proposed these two ideas in the same message that he sent to the Congress on 5 May

1993. And they were linked together conceptually, since he advocated not only community service, but also earning one's way to further education and training through performing such service. These two proposals then were severed and dealt with separately in the Congress, proceeding on quite different legislative tracks. But then, when both bills were in the final stages of decision making, they became intertwined again.

The community service bill passed the House of Representatives rather easily and moved to the floor of the Senate after being reported by the appropriate committee. In the full Senate a substitute was offered by Senator Kassebaum and was rejected, as she describes in her paper. But the Republican Senators did not give up and let the bill pass; they began a filibuster. As both Senator Kennedy and Senator Kassebaum suggest, the atmosphere of the times made it difficult for any Republican to cross the party line and support the new Democratic President's initiative. Yet no bill could pass the Senate without some votes from the Republicans, because the Democrats had only 57 votes and 60 were needed to cut off debate and pass the legislation.

As chance would have it, the final sessions of the Senate-House conference committee on the direct student loan program were occurring at the same time. Congressman Ford led a House delegation that insisted on a full conversion of the student loan program into a direct lending scheme, but the Senate delegation led by Senator Kennedy was divided. Senator Kennedy himself was a long-time advocate of the direct lending idea, having successfully secured Senate passage of that amendment in 1980 (only to see it fail in conference). But the rest of the Senate delegation was divided. Another prominent Democrat, Senator Pell, was opposed to a full-scale conversion, while Democratic Senator Paul Simon enthusiastically supported the idea. Senator Kassebaum, the leader of the Republicans, was opposed, as was Senator Jim Jeffords; but Republican Senator David Durenberger was solidly behind it.

The Senate had compromised in committee because of this split and advocated the idea of running parallel programs until the next reauthorization of the Higher Education Act in 1997. Lobbyists thought that Senator Kennedy might give in to the House during the House-Senate conference committee, since his own side was divided, he had long supported the idea, and the House seemed to be so adamant in its position.

The juxtaposition of a filibuster against the community service bill on the Senate floor and the final compromises that had to be made in conference on the direct lending concept meant that several Republican Senators became key in both situations. Senator Jeffords, for instance,

188

let it be known that he might be willing to vote to break the filibuster, but not if the Senate ceded to the House during the conference on direct lending. Consequently, Senator Kennedy had little choice; he needed those moderate Republican votes to secure approval of the President's community service bill.

The result was that the filibuster was broken and the community service bill was approved by the Senate; the Senate position of retaining two loan programs prevailed in conference (with some modifications). A short time later, Congressman Ford was quoted as saying that he hoped that what he had to agree to in conference on direct lending had at least kept the President's major community service initiative alive.

This interconnectedness of issues, sometimes on quite dissimilar questions, is not uncommon in Congress. Members of Congress often deal with legislative bills in a continuous flow, trading off support or opposition for unrelated reasons. In this instance, as it turned out, the issues were related.

To summarize, the lessons to be learned from the congressional consideration of these two bills are that the general atmosphere of the times has a notable, sometimes decisive influence on the outcome and that the particular manner in which a bill is presented also can have a determining effect. Last, for various reasons, the fate of bills becomes intertwined; and decisions on one can lead to trade-offs on another.

Individuals and Organizations

This series includes not only papers by Administration officials and by members of Congress, but also essays by various individuals and representatives of organizations who were influential in the decision making on these issues. Roger Landrum from Youth Service America is included because his voice was important in keeping the idea of community service alive during the years when it was not an important national issue; his efforts also laid the groundwork for the revival of interest in the concept in the 1990 legislation.

Thomas Butts was asked to write a paper because he revived the idea of direct lending after it had been debated and rejected in the late 1970s and early 1980s. As his opponent John Dean acknowledges, Butts was a tireless advocate; and his work directly led to the adoption of the demonstration program in the legislation in 1992 and then to the major shift in the loan program enacted in 1993.

The two other writers from private life were the opponents of the ideas advocated by Landrum and Butts. Doug Bandow was the critic of paid volunteerism who provided intellectual ammunition to the congressional forces fighting Clinton, Kennedy, and Ford. John Dean, an acknowledged expert on the intricacies of federal student aid, was the organizer of the bankers and other groups combating the shift to direct lending.

The campaigns in which these two opponents of Clinton's proposals engaged were quite different. The community service bill generated some concern from various groups, but the fight against the bill was mostly within the Congress. The direct lending proposal, on the other hand, led to a well-financed and well-organized battle involving people across the country.

Congressman Ford, Thomas Butts, and John Dean all refer to the pressures that were brought to bear on the latter issue. Ford talks about "heavy lobbying" and "special interests." Dean complains that Senator Simon used the congressional frank to send out mail generating support for the idea. Representatives and Senators were visited by bankers and representatives of their state guaranty agencies.

The explanation for the difference between the two battles is easy enough. Community service was a nice idea, and the creation of the program did not displace anything else. The only real concerns, apart from the politics of helping Clinton, were: 1) should volunteerism be paid and 2) should federal money be spent in this manner when the national government was running a deficit?

The direct lending concept was entirely different. It was clearly meant to replace one way of doing business with another. And it really was a "business" in that $18 billion a year was involved. Naturally, when someone is going to make less money, that person tends to act differently in opposition than if he or she merely disagrees conceptually with someone else's idea.

So the first lesson from the private groups' involvement is that one must know the nature of the interests involved in a dispute, whether they are financial or ideological, or both, before one can appreciate why certain arguments are made. I do not say this to denigrate anyone who is arguing for or against an idea and who has something to gain from the adoption of the new idea or from retaining the old way. Such people often best understand the system and must be relied on to explain the fallacies of the ideas. Rather, the point is that one must look behind the façade of any argument and try to understand the nature of the underlying interests.

The last lesson to be learned from the involvement of private groups in decision making in Washington is that the best insurance for the long-term retention of any policy is bipartisan support. Roger Landrum's paper betrays a nervousness about community service being identified as a Clinton initiative, and he stresses that the idea has a long history of support from both Democrats and Republicans. Landrum is right to be concerned. The country has a tendency to shift allegiances between the two political parties, and any policy too tightly bound to one party runs the risk of being abolished when the other party assumes power.

During the debate on direct lending, the advocates on the Democratic side who were fighting for Clinton's policy repeatedly made references to the support for the idea from Republican Congressmen and Senators, such as Tom Petri of Wisconsin and David Durenberger of Minnesota. The Democrats were trying to show that the policy, though advocated by a Democratic president, was not partisan. They realized that bipartisan sponsorship is a useful element to ensure the long-term survival of an idea.

Conclusion

The primary purpose of this book is to explain two major new national policies that will affect millions of Americans who pursue postsecondary education or training or who will be encouraged to perform community service. The secondary purpose is to use the enactment of these two laws as an occasion to understand how policy is made at the national level.

Many aspects of the decision making seem self-evident once they are described. But deriving these lessons from concrete events, such as the enactments of community service and direct lending legislation, may make them more understandable. For example, the general atmosphere of the times always has an effect on decisions, as it did with the community service bill. Knowing the philosophical bent or the financial interests of an advocate are part and parcel of understanding what motivates participants in the debate about the conversion of the student loan program into direct lending.

Few voters expect a politician to carry out every campaign promise, but the vote-getter will pay if promises are completely discarded after assuming office or if the general direction taken in the campaign later is ignored. That is why it was important for Clinton to enact some type of community service bill with a provision allowing volunteers to earn credit for a college education. Both Democratic and Republican members of Congress understood well the need for Clinton to achieve that goal.

Other points about the decision-making process may be less apparent. For instance, the budget deficit looms over every discussion in Washington; no President or member of Congress can ignore it in making legislative proposals. Further, the interconnectedness of issues is fascinating and not always visible to those who do not closely follow policymaking. Similarly, the form in which legislation is considered is vital to its fate. And finally, bipartisanship is essential to the continuity of policy; but since both parties are constantly looking for the advantage with the electorate, they often do not want to emphasize that point.

The American form of government is admired throughout the world for its openness to the opinions of its citizens. But since we are so used to this fact, we must constantly remind ourselves that our form of government works best when we all participate in it. It is my hope that this book will encourage a better understanding of our government and that citizens will therefore become more involved in making it work. National policies, such as the enactment of the community service and the direct lending legislation, will have an effect on millions of Americans. These policies are fashioned best when citizens fully enter into the debate.